TAIL GUNNER TAKES OVER

TAIL GUNNER TAKES OVER

FLIGHT LIEUTENANT RICHARD RIVAZ
D.F.C.

LUME BOOKS

LUME BOOKS

First published in 2021 by Lume Books
30 Great Guildford Street,
Borough, SE1 0HS

Copyright © Flight Lieutenant Richard Rivaz 1945

The right of Flight Lieutenant Richard Rivaz to be identified as the author of this work has been asserted by them in accordance with the Copyright, Design and Patents Act, 1988.

All rights reserved. No part of this publication may be reproduced, stored in a retrieval system, or transmitted in photocopying, recording or otherwise, without the prior permission of the copyright owner.

ISBN 978-1-83901-389-8

Typeset using Atomik ePublisher from Easypress Technologies

www.lumebooks.co.uk

To
CHAS. AND IVOR

Table of Contents

Part One
- Chapter I 3
- Chapter II 8
- Chapter III 16
- Chapter IV 22
- Chapter V 28
- Chapter VI 37

Part Two
- Chapter VII 47
- Chapter VIII 55
- Chapter IX 64
- Chapter X 71
- Chapter XI 81
- Chapter XII 88

Part Three
- Chapter XIII 95
- Chapter XIV 104
- Chapter XV 114
- Chapter XVI 122

Part Four
- Chapter XVII 131
- Chapter XVIII 141
- Chapter XIX 145
- Chapter XX 153

Epilogue 159

Postscript 161

Part One

Part One

Chapter I

"Have you seen anything of Jimmy?" I enquired.

"No... not since that amazing trip of his."

"What trip was that?" I asked my friend. "Tell me about it."

"Jimmy was near his objective searching for the target, when he was attacked by a night fighter which came in from below, unobserved by the tail gunner. The first burst, by some lucky chance... or unlucky, whichever way you take it... put the rear turret out of action, and the gunner could only sit and watch the fighter coming in.

"The fighter evidently realized what had happened, as there was no return fire from the tail. He made repeated attacks, flying all round their aeroplane, with Jimmy, of course, taking violent evasive action. Many of the attacks were from right underneath, and Jimmy said he could hear and feel the cannon shells hitting and bursting against their bombs."

"Expecting them to go off at any moment, I should imagine," I interrupted.

"Yes, but he didn't want to jettison them, as he was near the target, and was determined to bomb it, if he could possibly shake off the fighter which was still playing with them rather as a cat plays with a mouse.

"Jimmy said that, throughout, the tail gunner calmly sat and gave a running commentary on all that was going on, whenever the fighter was round their tail. Fortunately none of the crew was injured, although the aeroplane was pretty badly holed.

"After a bit, the fighter evidently exhausted all its ammunition and tried to formate on them, and then started flying all round them in circles. Eventually it became so cocky that it wrote itself off against their tail-plane."

"How do you mean?" I asked.

"Well, it actually tore off one of its wings by colliding with the tail-plane of their aircraft. It took most of one side of their tail-unit with it, of course, but in some incredible manner Jimmy brought it back."

"Who claimed the fighter?" I asked. "The pilot or the gunner?"

"I don't know," my friend replied. "The story ends there."

All hearsay... that was what I had to be content with after I left the squadron. Stories such as these, and I was always hearing them, were my only contact with my old life. They made me restless, almost jealous. I missed the life of the squadron; I missed my friends, the atmosphere of excitement, of uncertainty sometimes. I missed being on the spot and knowing what was happening. I felt out of it.

I was posted to on January 19th, 1942, on instructional work, intended as a rest from operations.

I had been with an operational squadron since August 1940 and it was with very mixed feelings that I left. I had made a lot of good friends on the squadron, and I hated the idea of leaving them: it meant starting a new life with a new type of work.

Incidentally, I knew I was in for a very much less pampered life. There is no doubt that when you are operating, you have more self-respect, and are treated as something of a hero... in fact, coddled and looked after rather like some valuable museum piece. You get the best of food, and why not? You never know when or where the next meal may be forthcoming, and you never know if the one you are eating may not be the last.

I did not mind the idea of instructing, so much as leaving the work I had joined the Air Force to do. There is all the difference, to my mind, between the instructing air crew - whether he be pilot, navigator, gunner, or any other form of flying man - and the operational air crew. Instruction, while being an essential duty, is after all only the means to an end, and I think most instructors want to reach that end themselves. Many, of course, like myself, are ex-operational flyers, but some have never been on an operational squadron, either through age, medical category, or some special instructional qualifications.

Most of the instructors I have met have wanted to get back - or transfer - to operational work. This, after all, is a very natural desire, as to fly and fight should be the aim of all who are flying in the Royal Air Force.

I had been flying as an air gunner for about eighteen months and during the last nine months of my time with the squadron I had been gunnery leader, with a certain amount of instructional work. I only flew on operations about twice, or maybe three times, a month, which is far less than the average *pilot* usually does.

In any case, the amount of flying one does is always dependent on the state of the weather, and is naturally far more in summer than in winter. Sometimes a week or more will go by without an aeroplane leaving the ground, except possibly for a local air test or something of that sort. Then, with a spell of fine weather, every aeroplane and aircrew will be active again.

As I said, my nerve was far from gone, although I was having to exercise considerable self-control at times to keep myself operationally fit. Some people can stand far more strain than others, which is obviously due to the make-up of the individual. Some people are blessed - or otherwise - with more imagination than others, and there is no doubt that imagination can play a big part in one's efficiency in the air.

It is the worrying beforehand that is the worst, when one's imagination can, if allowed to, run riot and cause a lot of misery and discomfort. I have always found that I have suffered far more distress before an operational trip, wondering what could and might happen, than on the actual trip itself, when usually I have been far too occupied to really worry. This does not mean that I have not been scared, because I have, and am not ashamed to admit it, or that I don't mind being shot at; because I do. I hate it! I often envy those stoical individuals who can carry on unperturbed under all conditions, no matter what happens. Either they have not such a vivid imagination as some, or else they have enormous powers of self-control... probably both.

No one can tell how they will behave or what their reactions will be when faced with real danger, until the actual moment arrives. There is no disgrace in being afraid: I suppose everyone who has flown operationally has been afraid at some time or another. In fact, I would call the man who says he has never been afraid, a liar. Fear, after all, is an instinctive reaction, assisting in self-preservation and as a warning against danger: as pain warns us our bodies are being hurt in some way, so fear warns us that danger is close.

There are of course degrees of fear. Some people are 'sick' with fear, or 'paralysed' with fear. I have seen both these cases, but I imagine they are comparatively rare. With some people fear quickens their actions and makes them more alert, while with others it is the reverse: their senses are dulled and their movements slowed down.

There is also the type of fear when death seems inevitable: I mean, of course, violent death, not natural death. I have twice experienced this sort of fear, but I think I would rather call it depression - a deep, grim depression - than fear. When I have been afraid in the air I have felt my heart pounding inside my chest, and my mouth has been very dry, but I have been very alert and conscious of my surroundings, deliberate in all my actions, and known all the time a sort of inner glowing of excitement. The feeling has passed with the departure of the danger. The cause has always been the proximity of danger, but not necessarily death... only death by some unlucky chance.

But when death has seemed almost inevitable, the feelings I have experienced have been excessive loneliness, a deep sense of depression, and a feeling of utter hopelessness and misery. Old people are not afraid to die, but with young people it is different: it is a complete severance from all we know and love, no matter what faith we may hold in the 'hereafter.' I have been very much afraid dozens of times, although I think I can safely say that I have never 'flapped,' and have never been in such a state that I have been unable to behave perfectly normally. I am not saying this in any sense of boasting, but merely stating a fact.

One of the few cases I remember of anyone asking to give up was that of a gunner who came to me while I was gunnery leader and asked if he could have a spell off operations. It was my job to know the flying history of all the gunners under my command, so I knew how many trips he had done and also the nature of those trips. I asked him why he wanted to go, but he would only give me vague and unsatisfactory replies.

I knew the man quite well, and there was certainly nothing windy or of a shirking nature about him. Eventually I had to resort to a threatening attitude, as he still maintained his requests to go.

In the end he said to me:

"It's my girl, sir. She's making herself ill with worry, and says that unless I give up flying she'll break off our engagement."

Well, this certainly explained a lot, and eased my mind considerably about the man himself, as I had felt convinced that he was not the type to give up easily. I explained to him that everyone on the squadron either had a girl, a wife, or a mother... someone who was worrying about him, and while it was hard on them and all that, they had to play their part by putting a brave face on it, and so on.

I gave him forty-eight hours leave, and told him to go and see his girl and try to drum some sense into her.

The first trip he did after he returned from his forty-eight, he got wounded in the leg. It was not a serious wound, but enough to keep him off flying for a month or two. When I reminded him that he would be getting a break after all, he grinned his hardest. I only hope his girl is worthy of him.

A lot of people would give anything to go on an operational trip. I know several very senior and elderly officers who have tried unsuccessfully: however senior you may be, there is always someone even more senior to say no!

But I do know one elderly Group Captain who sneaked off on a raid when he was supposed to be on leave, and without his wife's knowledge.

He did not return.

When his wife eventually heard he was safe, and a prisoner of war, she remarked: "He may be having a bad time where he is now, but I assure you it will be nothing to what he will get when he comes home!"

Chapter II

I hate saying good-bye, as I can never think of anything adequate to say. I went round visiting my friends just before leaving the squadron, making foolish remarks.

There was no one on the flying side who had been there when I joined: they had all either been posted, were missing, or had been killed. There are continual changes on an operational squadron, due, of course, to casualties and postings. I have been back since and have hardly known a soul, which I found rather depressing.

Often, of course, weeks go by without a squadron losing an aeroplane. Then that same squadron sometimes seems to have a run of bad luck, and several crews will go missing and their places will be taken by fresh ones.

There is no official mourning on a squadron when a crew is missing or killed. It is rotten luck, and everyone is very sorry - particularly, of course, the close friends of the unfortunate crew - but there is very little outward sign of grief. Life and the work of the squadron carry on uninterrupted.

If we started to mourn or show signs of grief, we should upset each other and our work and morale would be affected. In any case, it would not do any good: it would not bring back those who were missing.

As soon as a crew is reported missing or killed, their next-of-kin are immediately informed. The individual's kit is collected and carefully checked with great respect, usually by the padre or by some officer especially detailed and fitted for the job. It is always done immediately, so that the things are not left lying about, and there is no chance of anything getting lost.

I was once reported missing after we had ditched in the North Sea, and no word had been heard of us long after we were overdue. My next-of-kin received a telegram, and my belongings were collected and packed up. But I returned: '*One crew has since been reported safe…*' That was us!

Never before or since has my room been so tidy or my things in such good order! When it was known I was returning, the padre unpacked all my clothes and put them back, as he thought, where they belonged, but I could tell at a glance what had happened, as all my collars and handkerchiefs were in one drawer, socks in another, and so on, instead of all being jumbled together. I got great amusement from finding my things and muddling them all up again! Some of my letters are still tied in neat bundles, and I have not had the heart to undo them!

After I had been at for some time, people began to say how much better I looked, and that I appeared less tired, and so on.

Maybe this was so, but I personally think it was mostly imagination on their part, as I kept very fit whilst I was operating. I played squash most days in winter, and tennis nearly every day in the summer, and I made a point of getting all the fresh air and exercise I could - partly from the fact that I enjoy it, but also because there is no doubt that keeping really fit improves one's efficiency in the air. If you are fit, you feel less tired, and I am certain feel the cold less.

I used to drink a certain amount of beer, but never on the eve of the night I was operating. Not only is it confoundedly difficult to get rid of from a turret, but alcohol even in small quantities retards one's reactions and makes one more susceptible to the cold. One also needs more oxygen at high altitudes, with even a small amount of alcohol inside one.

I arrived at - with thick snow on the ground, which considerably increased my feeling of depression. I saw my days of luxury and comfortable living were over, as this was an aerodrome with wooden huts for mess and sleeping quarters. Oh, how I missed my old mess with its comfortable rooms, and which I had begun to look on almost as home.

I had an interesting enough job, though, with work I enjoyed. As regards hours it was a fairly light job, too. This suited me very well, as I was able to write *Tail Gunner*. I started the book in the middle, and not really with the idea of publication, but rather as a record for myself. I first wrote the story of ditching in the North Sea, and thought it was shaping rather well, so I continued with it and wrote round that story. I got infinite pleasure and interest out of the 'work,' and it was only want of time that prevented me from writing it more fully. Reading it through since, I have thought of all sorts of things I have wanted to add.

At my new job I was chief tactical instructor at an advanced gunnery course. My day consisted of one, or possibly two, lectures on tactics, as well as probably a certain amount of instruction in the air, both of which I enjoyed. I like lecturing when I know what I am talking about, and always get quite a thrill out of flying.

Sometimes Poles and Czechs were on the course, and came to my lectures. They were always very attentive, and usually took copious notes. I made a point of asking them if they could understand much English, and could they follow what I had been saying?

On one occasion I noticed a Czech officer sitting at the back of the room. He sat perfectly still, watching me intently throughout my lecture, and I was wondering the whole time how much he was able to understand. When I had finished talking, I went up to him and asked if he had understood. He replied in perfect English, and in the most courteous manner, that he was able to follow me perfectly well. I learnt afterwards that he could speak English as fluently and probably better than I could!

On another occasion there was a middle-aged Pole sitting right in the front. He, too, never took his eyes off me while I was talking, and again I had no indication as to whether he was able to understand the lecture. When I had finished, I asked him - could he understand?

He replied - "It does not matter. I have been lecturing on the same subject myself for the past twenty years in Poland."

We had a great number of air gunners passing through the school, and naturally I met some extraordinarily interesting people.

There was one gunner I remember particularly. He was very round-shouldered, and with a slight twist to his back. His hands, too, had obviously been badly damaged, and I noticed he had to hold his knife at meals dagger fashion. It was not long before I heard his story.

He had been gunner on some light type of aeroplane in India, which was attacked by a fighter, and during the combat the pilot was killed. The gunner did not bale out, thinking the pilot might not be dead, only wounded, but continued to fight back although the aeroplane was completely out of control. He eventually shot the fighter down just before they crashed.

When he woke up in hospital, he learned he had twelve bullet wounds in his body; that his back was broken in four places, and both wrists completely shattered. He had to have I don't know how many operations, and was in hospital well over a year. The doctors said he would never fly again, and only laughed at him when he said they were wrong.

Eventually he recovered his health, but was left with a somewhat mangled body. Still he was determined to fly, and if possible get back on to operations.

After much wangling, he persuaded the Medical Board to say that if he passed through this gunnery course, and showed that he was capable of operating a turret and stripping and assembling a gun as well as any normal man, they would pass him as A1 and fit for further flying. He worked like a nigger on the course, and passed out fourth from the top and with an excellent report from the C.O.

We had another gunner on the same course - an Irishman. At his medical he was told that he had a hammer toe, and could not be passed for flying duties. He said - "*Very well, then, take it off. Then will I be all right*"? He was assured that he would be, and had the offending toe removed. Some time later, he went up for another medical, and was told that as he had only nine toes, he could not possibly be passed for flying duties. However, he is in now and, as he puts it, has one less toe to get frost-bitten!

I used to spend a certain amount of time visiting squadrons, and collecting the latest tactical information. I liked this, as it meant flying in a number of different types of aircraft, which included *Stirlings, Halifaxes, Manchester, Blenheims* and *Beaufighters*.

I flew for a bit with Wing Commander Cunningham, or 'Cat's Eyes' Cunningham, as he is sometimes called. He is a night fighter pilot, and a charming person to fly with. I sat just behind him and could watch him handling his aeroplane, and his methods of interception, with great admiration.

I have never seen a pilot fly at night with less cockpit lighting. He dimmed all his instruments until they were barely visible, and he even had a mask over his illuminated compass which he removed only for a second or two when he wanted to check or re-set his course. By having so little light inside his aeroplane, he would have far better vision for searching the sky, and obviously decrease his chances of being seen himself. Once he has an enemy aircraft in his sights, it is good-bye to that aeroplane. I am glad he is on our side!

Another pilot I used to enjoy flying with was one of our staff pilots. We called him 'Bomber.' He was a Warrant Officer, and an Irishman with an Irishman's sense of humour and gift of the gab. He had over ten thousand flying hours to his credit, and I imagine knew practically all there was to know about flying. I have known no one handle an aeroplane with more skill and ease than he was able to.

At one time he had a run of bad luck which lasted about a week. He took the top off a tree whilst low flying - official low flying - but perhaps this was not bad luck! Another time his engine cowling came off in flight, and on still another occasion his aeroplane caught fire, but he managed to crash land it without injury to himself or his crew.

On each occasion he blamed the Gremlins. When his aeroplane caught fire he said he could see them running up and down the fuselage and the engines, striking matches as they went and giggling and nudging each other in their glee. When he took the top off the tree he said there were hundreds of the little brutes holding up the branches, and just as he passed overhead they pushed them up even higher. When his engine cowling came off, he said he could see them deliberately unscrewing it.

There has been a lot of talk about Gremlins, and a lot of rot talked, too. People have asked what Gremlins are, and do flying men really believe in them? What *are* Gremlins? Well, I will tell you. They are fairies - *naughty* fairies. Do you believe in fairies?

Sometimes I have been called on to talk to boys of the A.T.C. I always get a kick out of this, probably partly from the fact that they seem to enjoy the talks, and undoubtedly partly from the fact that they are a new audience and expect a good *line shoot*. You can pull them all your tallest stories - the taller the better - and even if they don't believe them, they pretend to and seem to enjoy them!

They always ask two questions. One is - '*Have you baled out?*'; and the other is - '*Have you shot down a fighter?*'

I always feel a bit of a worm when I have to answer - '*No*' - to the first question, but I make up for it by hastily adding that I have ditched twice! This does something to restore my respect in their opinion, which obviously drops very low when they learn I have never baled out.

Needless to say, I soon found an excuse to visit my old squadron.

On one occasion while I was there, I met the Duke of Kent. Although he was making an official call, he kept his visit as informal as possible, and chatted to many of us. I had not long before been shot down in the sea, and he asked to hear about it. He has been the most distinguished audience for my line-shooting stories so far!

Whilst I have been in the Air Force I have met many people of eminence and importance. I have been presented to the King, the Prime Minister, the Duke of Gloucester, and Sir Archibald Sinclair, as well as other notable personalities. On one occasion the King lunched at our mess. At his request the work of the station continued its normal routine while he was there, and many officers had started lunch before he arrived, as we were flying in the afternoon.

He entered the mess room accompanied by the C.O. and others, and I was immediately struck by his quiet dignity and vital personality. Although I never spoke with him, I felt I was not only in the presence of my King, but of a great and noble man.

The second time I was in the presence of the King was at Buckingham

Palace, when I received my D.F.C. Again I was impressed by his amazing personality. I felt while I was facing the King, that for the few seconds I was there, he gave me his whole attention - that I was the focus of his interest. This may sound a small thing, but when it is remembered that I was one of hundreds bowing, being spoken to, and shaken hands with by the King every few seconds, I think it was rather marvellous. I am certain others must have felt the same.

At this investiture there were, I imagine, about three hundred of us: Navy, Merchant Navy, Army, Air Force, as well as civilians, men and women. We were lined up, and when our names were called by the Lord Chamberlain we walked along a raised platform, to the accompaniment of light music in the background, and stood before the King.

Just before my turn came, the orchestra finished what it had been playing, and started on something new - *The Donkey's Serenade*! It was all I could do to compose my features into their normal serious expression before I approached His Majesty.

On two occasions I was a member of a crew that demonstrated the *Halifax* to the Prime Minister. We flew down to an aerodrome in the South of England, and parked our *Halifax* alongside other modern types of aircraft ready for inspection. The Prime Minister came along - complete with cigar, as we hoped he would - and I was particularly impressed by the power of the man... by his dominant personality and will. At that time the *Halifax* had not been in operation long, and was still giving some small teething trouble. The Prime Minister already knew about it, and immediately asked what was the cause of that trouble, what was being done to remedy it, and had the remedy worked? He examined the *Halifax* from the inside and demanded that I show him the working of the turret; and showed mock terror when I had the guns pointing in his direction. Sir Charles Portal was with him, and, as the Prime Minister moved off, the Air Chief Marshal lagged behind talking. Mr. Churchill called back to him: "Come here, Portal, I want to talk to you."

The Duke of Gloucester visited us an hour or two after our aerodrome had been bombed. I did not know he was there until I saw him standing with a group of others in the mess, or rather what was left of it!

Sir Archibald Sinclair arrived by air one day, and had a talk to aircrews waiting for him in the Crew Room. He asked me about conditions in my turret. Had I leg room? What was the visibility like? Was there any heating? To the first question I answered 'Yes'; to the second '*Good*'; and to the third - NO!' When he speaks to you he stands very close and holds you with his eyes, which are almost magnetic in their concentration and power.

Chapter III

I must now mention Lockie. She is my bull terrier, and has the most lovable nature of any dog I have ever known. She is now sixteen months old, and I have had her since she was five weeks.

I collected her, looking rather like a little shivering pink pig, from York, and drove her back to the aerodrome tucked inside the top of my tunic, which I soon found to be the most convenient method of carrying her about with me. She had a strong objection to walking... and anyway, progress was so slow when she *did* walk, as she either fell over every few seconds, or else sat down.

Quite early in her career, when she was about three months old, I lost her. She walked out of my office in the company, as I thought, of a colleague; but I did not worry, as I thought he was taking her for a walk as he often did.

When he returned without her the search party started. I had every available man in the squadron searching, and whistling, and calling, but to no avail. I was nearly frantic, imagining all the awful things that might have happened to her. To make matters worse it was getting dark, and almost time for briefing, as we were due out on a daylight raid the following day.

Briefing time arrived but no Lockie.

Suddenly I thought of the *Tanoy*. The Tanoy is a system of loud speakers distributed throughout the aerodrome, through which urgent news such as air raid warnings, important messages to personnel, and so on, are broadcast. I rushed into the Ops. Room, on my way to briefing, with a request that an SOS be sent out for Lockie.

The C.O. was just giving us our target when his voice was drowned by '*Attention everyone... attention everyone.*' - blaring through the loud speaker over his head. He stopped, and everyone listened.

'*Will anyone who has seen the bull terrier pup belonging to Flying Officer Rivaz hold the dog and ring the Ops. Room immediately? Ten shillings reward is offered for the safe return of the dog. Message ends*'

The C.O. continued his briefing, with a glare in my direction. He had already spent some time searching his office premises!

A message was handed to me as I came out of briefing, saying that Lockie was having tea in the Sergeants' Mess.

During the winter months many aircrews take regular sun-ray treatment. I used to have my dose every afternoon and took Lockie with me. The dark glasses fitted her quite well, and she used to sit beside me, facing the light and turning as I turned. She became even pinker about the nose and tummy!

The C.O. became very fond of her, and allowed her in the mess. One evening we were sitting round the fire with our tankards of beer, and the C.O., Robby, had put his tankard - a full pint one - on the floor beside him. Presently we heard a lapping sound, and looked down to see Lockie with her nose in the beer.

Robby did not mind a bit. He looked at his watch and timed her. One minute, ten seconds... and the tankard was empty!

Lockie then tripped round the room, leering at all of us in turn. She finally finished up at Robby, sat down in front of him, gazed affectionately up into his face, and let off the most beautiful belch! For the remainder of the evening the steward was kept busy mopping up pools!

I did not take Lockie into the air with me until she was about nine months old, as I did not think it would be particularly good for her. The first aeroplane I took her in was a *Hudson*, on air firing exercises. She took it all as a matter of course, and showed no interest until the guns were fired. This she thought was great fun, and rushed up and down the fuselage in her excitement, wondering what it was all about and where the noise was coming from.

It was suggested tactfully to me after this that I did not make a habit of including Lockie in flying details. Since then she has only flown when I have been travelling by air, and has been in a *Halifax*, *Wellington*, *Hampden*, and *Lysander*, and has always shown the same boredom as she does in a car or a train.

She always attended all my lectures, and expressed her boredom in the most obvious ways. She used to sit still as long as she could, and then began to run round the room, surreptitiously pulling handkerchiefs out of pockets and eating pencils that happened to be unguarded; finally rushing round the room shaking the blackboard duster and covering everyone with white chalk. If I lacked for entertainment in my lectures, I think Lockie made up for it!

She accompanies me wherever I go, whether I am on duty or on leave, and at this moment she is sitting beside me. When she enters a railway carriage she leaps straight away on to the most comfortable lap she can find. This is a little embarrassing at times, particularly if that lap should belong to a Lieutenant-General, as happened on one occasion!

When I first had Lockie she felt the cold a lot, so I used to let her sleep in my bed. This is a habit of which I have never been able to break her, though I must say I have not tried very hard! When she was small there was no difficulty about this at all, but now, with her forty odd pounds, it is a very different story. However, with plenty of practice I have developed a technique, both for lying still and turning over. The only way is to have her with her back against my chest: this keeps her legs out of the way, and prevents violent kicking in the night. When we turn, she rolls over on top of me and takes up the same position on the other side.

On one occasion, a female cousin asked if she might have Lockie for warmth one night. I reluctantly but generously allowed this. I am pleased to say my cousin woke up on the floor!

Having so little work to do, I was often let in for a variety of odd jobs, and one day I was called upon to act as pall bearer at a funeral. I saw my name on D.R.O.'s the day I got back from leave, to officiate that very afternoon.

I had never done anything of the sort before, and there was no time for a rehearsal. I contacted my fellow bearers, and found them as ignorant as myself.

One thing we all agreed on at once, though, and that was that our varying sizes would not help matters at all. I am just over six foot; another man was six foot three; another one hardly more than five foot, while two more were about five foot seven.

There should have been six of us, but the sixth man had not read D.R.O.'s, and was flying when he was wanted. We did not discover this until just before it was time to set out for the funeral, and too late to get a substitute.

None of us knew the man who had been killed… how big or how heavy he was, but we thought we could manage with four, and that it would be better for the odd man to drop out. The obvious one to do this, of course, was the smallest one among us.

In due course we were taken to where the coffin was lying. The coffin was resting across trestles, a couple of feet or so from the ground, and covered by a Union Jack.

After saluting and standing at attention for a few moments, we approached the coffin. There was then some whispered discussion and disagreement as to whether we should remove our hats before we shouldered our burden, or keep them on our heads. We eventually took them off, as we thought they would probably get knocked off anyway.

We arranged that the two tallest should take the head and the other two the foot end of the coffin. We then bent our knees to a crouch position and crept underneath with the coffin resting on our shoulders.

At a whispered word we straightened our legs, or rather, tried to, but they would not move. We were held down by some immovable weight. We strained but with no avail, and had to relax again for a further whispered discussion. The deceased must have been an outsize in pilots, and we were straining beneath a load beyond the capabilities of four men to lift.

Well, we had to get the coffin on to the lorry waiting outside, somehow, so we had one more try. By terrific straining and some gigantic effort we just managed to raise it, and staggered with our load to the waiting conveyance, the floor of which was about shoulder height, so we had no great difficulty in transferring our burden to the required position.

We next had to slow march to the cemetery - about a mile away - two of us on either side of the coffin.

I had not gone far when I got a stone in my shoe... one of those small sharp stones that creep inside and work round until they find where they will hurt most. The temptation to stop and put a finger inside my shoe became almost unbearable: it would have been only a matter of seconds to stop, stoop, and insert a crooked finger inside to remove the offending jagged piece of rock, but I could not. There was nothing I could do but carry on and hope for the best.

We arrived at our destination after what seemed like an interminable route march, and once more shouldered our load and staggered for the remainder of the journey with the coffin sloping at an alarming angle towards the front.

When we reached the graveside, where there were a couple of beams of wood across the top of the grave on which we had to rest the coffin, we realized that the most complicated part of our job was about to begin. How were we to transfer our burden, which seemed to be pressing me into the ground, with due reverence and in a manner suited to the solemnity of the occasion, from our shoulders to its desired resting place?

The problem was solved for us in no uncertain manner, and in a way we least expected. My partner, while manoeuvring into position on the edge of the grave, trod on my foot. I said something I should not have said on consecrated ground, and withdrew my foot to a safer place. My partner, in his confusion, trod too near the grave, the edge of which gave way, and in he went! The coffin came down with an awful bang on to the wooden rests, but luckily without apparent damage.

We pulled my partner out of the grave, and the service began.

Nothing untoward occurred until the very end, when further respects were paid by firing a salute. On the command - 'Load' - there was a loud report, as one of the rifles accidentally went off! I involuntarily relaxed my position of attention and glanced in the direction of the offender, and immediately wished I had not, as the rifle was pointing directly at me!

Another job I sometimes had to do was to take a *charge*. It was a job I hated doing, as I always felt so sorry for the culprit.

When an airman commits an offence he is put *on charge* and brought under escort before the officer under whose particular command he happens to be. When you take a charge the airman is marched before you. You read his offence out in front of him, ask him if he has anything to say, cross-question witnesses, if any, and eventually pronounce sentence. It is all taken very seriously, whether the offence be petty or great.

On one occasion I had an airman before me who had missed parade and used improper language to the corporal whose job it was to rout him out. Like a fool, I asked the corporal what the man had said.

He certainly had a wonderful vocabulary! It was all I could do to keep a straight face, and glanced at the flight-sergeant standing beside me. He was gazing at the offender with obvious admiration!

Often we used to have visiting officers stopping at the mess, either for a meal or for a few nights. I sat next to one of these officers one day at tea, and I thought he looked very old to be in the Royal Air Force, even on the ground, so could not resist asking him if he ever had the opportunity to fly? His reply was:

"Young man, my grandfather would not go in a train; my father would not go in a motor car, *and I am certainly not going in an aeroplane*"

Chapter IV

I suppose everyone looks forward to leave: I know I do. I don't like towns for more than a few days, and usually spend most of my leave in the country... usually, on a farm. I do odd jobs if I feel like it, or else just laze about. My farmer friends are very interested in aeroplanes and the ways of aeroplanes, and I usually have to answer innumerable questions.

I always think aeroplanes in flight are such impersonal things. It seems hard to realize that they contain individuals: men feeling, thinking, laughing and talking, conscious of the ground and yet free from it. The aeroplanes look so small; almost insignificant; sometimes seemingly unreal, yet when you are flying in them they are very real; they are your world, your very life. At a touch or a movement of your hands and feet they respond: you are master of the air, and they are your medium.

It is one of the most exhilarating things I know, controlling an aeroplane. There is no limit. On the road you are limited by a narrow strip of tarmac; on the sea you are bound by the surface of the water: but in the air... in the air there is no limit. You are free: you can go up; you can go down, or to either side; climbing, diving, turning, side-slipping, rolling and spinning; there is no limit. Man can do that which for centuries past he has only been able to watch and envy the birds doing. In flying there is rhythm, beauty and movement.

There is beauty on a farm, too, a simple, unsophisticated, satisfying sort of beauty. It is unhurried. It can afford to wait, as it is always there: everywhere you turn, it is waiting for you.

There is the rickyard, with one rick partly cut and the hay knife stuck in with only the handle showing, and a ladder resting against the side. There is the wood pile against the barn. There is the cart shed; you can just see the carts in the half gloom, with their shafts resting on the ground.

But this is all a passive beauty, without movement. It is the beauty of age and tranquillity. It is a sedative, and I hope it will never change.

There is movement, too.

Look at the chickens scratching in the dung mix, and the fat-bellied ducks pushing their bills through the mud. They are alive, and their beauty is always changing.

Look at the cows pulling at the grass. See their shape and colour: how they walk, with their heads down, eating as they go, or move with slow, swinging movements, swishing their tails and gazing about them with their large, melancholy eyes.

See the farmer beneath his pitch of hay, walking with leisurely stride towards the stable.

Away on the brow of the hill, the ploughman strides behind his team, with head tilted to one side. He looks content, and I am sure he is happy.

It is all beauty and purpose.

Farmers are supposed to be proverbial grumblers, but I must say I have not noticed it myself. My farmer - I call him *my* farmer, as I spend so much of my leave there - never grumbles. His crops may grow and do well and his cows may produce their maximum milk: then he will smile. His crops may be wilted with frost or drought; his cows may sicken and fall off with their milk, but he will not grumble: he knows he has done the best he can; he has done his job, and complaining will not help. There is a lot of truth in the old proverb - *It is no good crying over spilt milk*. I have got no time or patience, or any sort of use, for grumblers. To my mind it is one of the most despicable traits anyone can have. They do no one any good, and should be out of the way where they can do no further harm.

A farmer lives as intimately with nature as it is possible to live: he must study her, and usually bow down to her. We have yet to conquer the elements: probably we never shall.

The flyer too, in a sense, lives near to nature. He is often alone in the clear, clean air... air purer than can ever be found near the ground. The weather can be his enemy or his friend: he must learn, as the farmer does, to watch the weather and use it to his advantage, or to shun it as a foe.

Fog and ice are the airman's greatest enemies. I know one pilot who said to me: "*I don't mind flak; I can cope with that, but I can't cope with ice.*" Ice can be the means of destruction of an aeroplane as quickly as any foe: it forms on the surfaces in a few seconds, and can be really dangerous. Not only will it add great weight to the wings, but also it will upset their shape and make them no longer capable of the job for which they were designed; or it may completely jam the controls. If an aeroplane gets really badly iced it will stall and immediately come out of control, and will probably crash.

Icing conditions are met with both in clouds and below clouds, and the pilot must know how to recognize these particular clouds and how to avoid them. Of course, most aeroplanes are now fitted with devices to prevent this icing up, but sometimes conditions are so severe as to make these gadgets practically useless.

One day when I was on leave, I ran into Hinks; whom I had not seen for some time. He was a middle-aged, grey-haired man, and if you did not know him you might think he had some sedate, quiet job on the ground. But you would be wrong. He had been a pilot during the last war, and he joined up for this war as an air gunner.

"How are you getting on?" I asked. "Have you had any excitement lately?"

"Well... I don't know," he replied. "I suppose in a way... "

He was like that: he would never give a direct answer, but was always very cautious in his speech as well as in what he did, and needed a lot of prompting to talk about himself.

"Let's hear all about it," I said. "We'll go and have a drink."

"Well... "he began, when we were comfortably settled. "We were on a trip to Hamburg. There was the usual flak over there, and, as you know, it's a pretty hot target; but we dropped our bombs without anything unusual happening, and were well on the way home when we were held in a cone of searchlights. They formed a ring all around us: it was like looking at a dazzling wall of light which always kept its distance from us and moved as we moved.

"There were a few searchlights on to us as well, which nearly blinded me in the rear turret. There was no flak at all, so it was obvious that there were fighters about.

"As you can imagine, I was straining for all I was worth into this dazzling light, and sure enough a fighter loomed up behind. He was firing when I saw him, as a massive black shape which must have been within a hundred yards. I opened up immediately, but could not see what had happened. He disappeared, and his place was almost instantly taken by another. There were five of them altogether. I fired at them all: I don't know how many rounds I fired... pretty nearly all I'd got, I think."

"Did you shoot any down?" I interrupted.

"Well... it's hard to say: I wouldn't like to say definitely *yes*"

"I bet you did!" I said.

"Well, I certainly saw my tracer going through them," he answered. "But you know what it's like when you're pretty near blinded by searchlights: unless they actually burst into flames you can't tell what's happened. All the time the pilot was obviously doing everything he could to get clear away by taking violent evasive action."

"Was there any damage done?" I asked.

"Yes; Roy, the front gunner, was badly wounded: he had a cannon shell burst in the turret, which practically took off his arm. Another one burst in the cockpit, blowing out most of the instruments, and we had a tank badly holed. Also my turret was put out of action, but not until the very end, thank God!"

"You're a lucky old blighter, you know, Hinks," I remarked.

"Wait a minute, I haven't finished yet," he went on. "Our first job, of course, was to get Roy out of the front turret. It was an appalling job, I can tell you.

"He was more or less unconscious, and you know what a job it is at the best of times, moving about an aeroplane. It took us about an hour - I was working with Geoff, the second pilot - to get him back on to the bed. When we eventually got him back I was so exhausted, probably from lack of oxygen, that I could only lie across him for a few moments.

"He was part of the time conscious, and part of the time out. Of course we gave him morphia, and applied a tourniquet, and did our best to keep him warm, which was not easy, as it was bloody cold in the fuselage. I spent the rest of the trip with him, doing anything I could to make him comfortable.

"As we reached the German coast, Geoff told me that we had lost about three hundred gallons of petrol, and there was no chance of getting back. Obviously we did not tell Roy how we were fixed.

"Roy would not allow me to leave him for a second. He was only about nineteen, and was certainly marvellous. At times he thought he was going to die, and left all sorts of messages for his mother and his girl; and at times he asked me if he was going to die, and implored me not to let him. He seemed to look on me as a father, and at times, I think, thought that I was: it was my grey hairs, I suppose.

"Well, there we were, wondering how far we should get. There was a bit of doubt about the exact amount of petrol we had left, but Geoff said we had definitely lost about three hundred gallons.

"I wondered how - when we baled out - we should get Roy out of the aeroplane. He obviously could not jump himself. I considered jumping with him, but thought our parachutes might get tangled, so I tied a long cord to the ripcord of his parachute, and was going to fasten the other end to the structure near the exit when the time came.

"When we got over Holland, the pilot estimated we still had another fifteen minutes' petrol left, and asked the crew which they would rather do… bale out over there, or make straight across the sea and take a chance on ditching? We decided without much hesitation on the latter.

"Well, we headed straight across… all of us looking anxiously at our watches. The pilot decided to carry on until the engines cut, and then bring her down. It was the longest quarter of an hour I ever remember, sitting there, waiting and wondering how far we should get.

"Roy was marvellously patient. He must have been in terrible pain at times, but he never complained. When he was conscious he talked quite a lot, and was pathetically grateful for anything I could do for him, which, God knows, wasn't much.

"Well… you can imagine how we sat during that quarter of an hour: looking at our watches, listening to the engines, and waiting for them to splutter.

"The time was up, and we were still flying! The petrol gauges had read zero for some time, so we had no idea what was left. We were still flying, and we continued on towards the coast.

"To cut a long story short, in some miraculous way the petrol held out. As we sighted an aerodrome the engines cut, and the pilot brought her straight in without troubling about the wind, to make a crash landing."

"What happened to Roy?" I asked.

"They had to cut away the side of the fuselage to get him out, but he died in the ambulance."

Chapter V

After I had been at for about eight months, I had a signal from the Air Ministry asking if I still wanted to take a pilot's course. I was overjoyed, as it was what I wanted to do above everything else.

I had put in for the course about eighteen months prior to this, but as I had not heard, I imagined nothing would come of it, and had almost forgotten about it.

But with this reminder my enthusiasm started afresh. It would mean a course for the best part of a year, probably... training, and with no prospect of promotion during that period, but neither of these thoughts worried me in the least. It would mean saying good-bye to more friends, and it would mean meeting and making fresh ones, and I must confess neither of these worried me much either. I felt very selfish in my desire to be a pilot.

I originally intended joining the Royal Air Force as a pilot, but there was some considerable delay for that, although at the time there was a demand for air gunners; so I decided to take what was going, and went straight in as an air gunner.

I have not regretted my action one atom. I have learnt a lot, seen a lot, made a lot of good friends, had some excitement, and although I cannot claim to equal St. Paul in his experiences, nevertheless I have certainly had some interesting times. But I want some more.

No, I have never regretted being an air gunner, but I am quite ready for a change, and I do want to be a pilot. I have been flown for several hundreds of hours by other people: I have been a passenger... a stooge, with only occasionally a chance to act. Now I want to be the boss: I want to have control.

Not that I disliked being an air gunner, or that I mistrusted my pilots... far from it; but I wanted to pilot myself for a change. I have always disliked being a passenger in a car, and liked whenever possible to take the driver's seat. I consider myself rather a good driver! This does not mean, necessarily, that I will make a good pilot. One of the best pilots I know is a shockingly bad car driver. I would go anywhere with him in an aeroplane, and have been to many places - including Berlin - but I hate going even half a mile with him when he is driving a car!

It was with a very light heart that I went about my duties from the time I heard from the Air Ministry, until the day came for me to go. My colleagues were full of envy, as most of them had been trying unsuccessfully to get away from instructional work and back to operations. True, I would not be operational for a very long time, but I was on the way there, and I would rather wait and be an operational pilot, than an operational air gunner straight away.

I was told I was a lucky dog, and had all the good fortune, but I only laughed and said their turn would come soon. I was delighted, and I showed it.

Some of my gunner friends called me *traitor*: said I was deserting them, that I had no right to, that I was an air gunner and should be content to stay an air gunner. Think of all the training I had had as such: think of my experiences and what I knew.

But again I only laughed. I did not care a bit: I wanted to be a pilot, and anyway, they were probably jealous!

I wanted a crew, and the responsibility of a crew. I wanted to be able to say '*Yes*' or '*No.*' As an air gunner I always had to fly under the command of the captain of an aeroplane, and always envied him his job... a job worth learning, continually practising, and a job very necessary to be good at. But I wanted more: I wanted the most important job of all... to be the captain of an aircraft with a crew of my own; a crew who would look up to me, trust me, and who would depend on me for their safety.

I know and have flown with so many first-class captains; and because they were good captains they had good crews. The crews were set a high standard, knew a high standard was expected of them, and in consequence gave that high standard.

When the best is expected of a person, that person nearly always gives of the best.

When I realized that my pilot's course had at last come through, my first reaction was... bomber pilot. I would be a bomber pilot with my own crew. I am not afraid of responsibility, and have not much use for the person who is. I would rather make a decision myself than have to depend on someone else, unless that person should be more qualified to make it than I would be.

A gunner friend said to me: "How will you feel with someone else in the tail? Do you think you will trust anyone else there?"

Well, I should be a miserable sort of creature if I did not. But I should be mighty particular whom I had there, and probably a very hard task-master; but I should be very sympathetic! I am not sure that I envy that person very much!

I would rather be a bomber pilot working with a crew than a fighter pilot working single-handed. It is the crew working together, the 'crew spirit,' that is so important on a bombing raid: and anyway, it is the type of flying I know and understand.

So often you hear over the wireless, or read in the papers, that our pilots saw this or did that. This always annoys me so. Why 'our pilots'? Why not 'our crews'? It is all right to say 'our pilots' when referring to single-seater fighters, but not when referring to bombers. The bomber pilot would be nowhere without his crew.

Granted, the responsibility of reaching the target, making decisions, and bringing the aeroplane back, rests with the pilot; but without his crew he could do none of these things.

It is impossible, really, to say who is the most important man in a crew. There are times when the aeroplane would never get back were it not for the navigator, and the navigator alone. There are times, when an aeroplane is lost, that were it not for the wireless operator getting fixes and loop bearings, that aeroplane would stay lost. The whole crew's safety would depend on him. There are times, when an aeroplane is attacked by fighters, that were it not for the gunner or gunners shooting down or driving off the fighters, the bomber itself would be shot down.

I can recall at least two occasions on which our aeroplane would not have got back were it not for me. Who was the most important member of our crew then? Why, *me*, of course! I nearly wrote 'person' instead of 'member of our crew,' but if I had said 'person' I should have referred to an individual, whereas I intended to refer to a tail gunner… any tail gunner.

On many trips I could have been dispensed with altogether, though no one was to know this before we set out; but on the two occasions I have in mind, nothing the pilot could have done on his own would have brought our aeroplane back to its base.

Under all these conditions, all the pilot can do is to go on flying, trust his crew, and leave them to play their part and do all that is necessary.

There is no doubt at all that crew co-operation is essential for the successful completion of an operational flight. It is the crew working together and in harmony, each man knowing thoroughly and doing efficiently his own particular job and having complete confidence in his fellow, that is so important.

There is often keen crew competition on a squadron: which crew would be the most successful?… which crew would bring back the best target photographs and have the best bombing results?… and so on. Most crews have great respect for their captains, and most captains are very proud of their crews.

As the days for me to start my pilot's course drew near, my enthusiasm increased. I saw myself captain of my own crew. I began picking who my crew would be: I even began talking to them in my day-dreams. I realized I had been sinking into a groove while instructing, and I needed this course to pull me out.

I make no apology for so much repetition of the word 'crew'; it is only what I feel.

I said farewell to another phase of my life and work, and went to an

I.T.W. where I learnt the elements of navigation; how to lay a course, plot a fix; the difference between a compass course, magnetic course, and true course; how to convert wireless bearings to a course by the Abac scale; how to use a computer; the difference between courses and tracks, air speeds and ground speeds; when to use the mercator chart and when to use the gnomonic chart, and how to map read from a polyconic. I learnt about compass turning errors and why they occur, and how the A.S.I. and altimeter function.

I was taught the elements of meteorology: how to recognize different clouds, and what weather conditions to expect from them; how the winds blow; the difference between warm and cold fronts, and when icing occurs; how to read weather maps, and what stars to use for navigation.

I attended lectures on the principles of flight and why the aeroplane flew. All very elementary, but very necessary. I attended lectures on signals and armament both of which I already knew: I went to lectures on gas, which I thought I knew, but did not: I did drill and P.T., both of which I enjoyed.

I kicked myself dozens of times while I was doing this navigation, for not having taken more interest in it when I had had the opportunity. On scores of occasions I have watched the navigator plot a course on his chart: on innumerable occasions I have had the chance while in the air to study the navigator at work. I have heard him give the pilot changes of course; talk about fixes and bearings, courses and E.T.A.'s... but I had been content to sit and listen, and, just because it was not my particular job, took it all for granted. More fool I!

Well, we live and learn, and I was having to learn a jolly sight harder now, because of my previous laxity. It was not that I thought that navigation was the prerogative of the navigator: I knew perfectly well that it is just as much the responsibility of the pilot, but it was just that I was too lazy to trouble to learn, thinking that I should never need it. Again, more fool I!

I was back at school again, and I enjoyed it. Although my hours of working were far longer than I had been used to, I felt as though I were having a rest. It was the change and entire lack of responsibility.

My sole responsibility was to see that I was not late for parade, and was on time for lectures. Everything was thought of and done for me. I was told when to get up, what I must wear, when I must eat, where I had to go, what I must do: and I liked it... for a bit!

One thing, however, worried me a whole lot, and that was my utter ignorance of mathematics. I had completely forgotten everything I had ever learnt at school, which, granted, was never very much! I could add, and I could subtract, but that was about all! I knew I should have to reach a higher standard than this, for navigational purposes, and I wondered if I should ever get there; but I need not have worried, as the instructors were so excellent: they must have been, as I passed my examinations!

Our instructors took it for granted from the start that we knew nothing, and in most cases they were perfectly right. They started at the very beginning, and took us patiently through. I passed my examinations, and I can pay them no better tribute!

Looking back, I thoroughly enjoyed the course, though I groused a lot, as most of us did. After a bit I began to kick at being treated like a schoolboy, and was impatient to start flying; but on the whole I really enjoyed myself, and once more I made some good friends.

This I.T.W. was by the sea, in a very delightful part of the country. The weather was good, and we bathed. There was also some good tennis, and some golf, and life on the whole was very pleasant.

While I was there I saw from the ground for the first time an aeroplane shot down: I had seen them shot down from the air before, but never from the ground. I had seen several crashes but unfortunately those of our own machines. This was a *Focke-Wulfe* 190 which came over one evening while we were playing tennis; dropped its bombs, and machine-gunned us.

While it was overhead it suddenly broke into flames... great long, red flames which spread the entire length of the fuselage. It towered vertically for about fifteen hundred feet, stalled, and then went straight down in a dive and crashed on the beach a few hundred yards from where we were. This rather compensated us for the scare we had had a few seconds before!

Before our course came to an end, we had a dance in the mess. I hate a crowd and noise; they give me a feeling of claustrophobia, and I am not much of a one for dances; but I attended this one partly from a sense of duty, and chiefly because I could think of no excuse to get out of it.

The success of a mess dance naturally depends to a certain extent on the female element, and in having enough ladies to go round, as it were. I think they rather overdid it this time, though, as there appeared to be several unattached ladies in the earlier part of the evening. They were standing round in twos and threes, and appeared rather out of it.

I approached one of them and asked her if she would care to dance. She replied: "That's what I came here for."

And that is what she did for the next three hours! We waltzed, and we foxtrotted; we polka'd, and we did all sorts of dances I knew nothing about; in fact, danced the whole evening. I could think of no reasonable excuse to get rid of her. I could not say I was booked for the next dance, as I knew no other ladies there; and I could not very well say I was bored and wanted to go to bed, which would have been true.

About half-way through the evening we had a *Paul Jones*, and I thought my chance of escape had at last arrived. We automatically separated for this, and I joined the ring of men and skipped round the room.

I thought I would dance them all, and then slip unobtrusively off to bed before the last one had finished, but I miscalculated somewhat and found myself dancing with my original partner once again. I did not take much note of this until the band had stopped, when I realized with a shock that the dance had ended and that I was landed once more with my tenacious partner. I clapped the band frantically, hoping for an encore, but no, they would not strike up again.

The band had had enough, and so had I! I had lost my chance of escape, and resigned myself to boredom for the remainder of the evening with my tenacious and rather terrifying partner. Probably she was as bored as I was!

I passed my examinations all right, and, what pleased me, without cheating! I had every intention of cheating if it would get me through, as I knew the stuff perfectly well: I was not going to allow examination room nervousness to prevent me attaining my ambition of becoming a pilot. I was bristling with cribs, and I had no compunction about having a peep at them if they were to be my only means of getting through!

But I did not have to. I did not peep once!

If the examination had been competitive; if any serious issue had been at stake, except to myself, I should not have even contemplated cheating, but as we were at war, and I was determined to fly... well!

Before going overseas for the flying part of our training, we had to pass what was known as a grading test. The idea of this was to see if we could really fly, and if we would be worth training. There is no doubt that some people will never make pilots, just as some people will never be able to drive a car decently. It is largely a question of temperament, combined, of course, with a certain skill.

This course consisted of a required number of hours on *Tiger Moths*. The weather was in our favour while we were doing our flying, and we passed out in just over a fortnight.

The uncomfortable thought was with me before I started... *Suppose I could not fly after all? Suppose I could not land the plane? Suppose I was too heavy-handed and could not co-ordinate my movements to those necessary to be able to fly?* It might be so. I could not tell.

True, I had handled a *Halifax* and a *Wellington* on several occasions while they were in the air, but this was very different from landing an aeroplane and taking one off. Well, I should soon see. I should soon know if I was able to fly.

I had an officer instructor whom I liked, although he used to annoy me very often in the air. He talked continuously in a high-pitched voice, which soon became very monotonous. He talked about air dynamics, and what was happening to the aeroplane when in flight; he talked of *lift* and *drag*, and used to describe the airflow over the wings when the aeroplane stalled; what happened in a flat turn; why you should not use too much rudder when turning at low speeds... and so on. I was far more interested when I was off the ground in how to handle the aeroplane when she stalled, and how to put on bank when gliding. I was not interested in what was happening to the airflow; I could learn all about that in the lecture rooms, but while I was flying I wanted to concentrate on the best means of doing so.

But I must not grumble. I am very grateful to him, as he taught me a lot and got me through my tests with quite high marks. On our first outing he showed me how to taxi... told me why I should use ailerons as well as rudder when taxi-ing when there was a wind; showed me the best flying speeds, and the general capabilities of the aircraft.

There was no novelty for me in being in the air; I was not interested in the ground, as beginners are. But I *was* interested in the controls: in what was the best speed for climbing, cruising, gliding; how the rudder was used with ailerons in a turn, and what engine revs were used for the varying attitudes of flying. I was there to learn, and I absorbed it all eagerly: it was something new.

Up to then I had taken flying an aeroplane more or less for granted. I had trusted myself to those who knew how. But now I was no longer to be a passenger: I was to fly myself, and I intended to fly well. I was thrilled to be in the air again after about three months on the ground, and still more excited to be flying myself.

My instructor was very keen on aerobatics, and I think he was rather glad to have someone with him who did not mind his doing them. Nearly always before we came down, he used to say: *'Are your straps tight? I'm going to do a roll.'* - or - *'I'm going to loop'*

The first time I did a spin I was a bit dubious as to whether I should like it... but I thoroughly enjoyed it. The *Tiger Moth* seems to spin at an incredible rate of turn, and you get the impression while looking down that the ground is on some gigantic disc which is rotating below you. When you right the aeroplane, the disc ceases to revolve and becomes stationary; the horizon comes into view, and everything assumes its normal aspect. It is great fun, and there is no feeling of your boots being fixed to the floor, or of a great weight being pressed upon you, or of your eyes being drawn out of your head, as you get in many air manoeuvres.

Chapter VI

There was keen competition among a group of us as to who would go solo first... and more by luck than anything, I was the first to go. Not that I think I was learning to fly quicker than the others, or was any better than they were, but I think because my instructor was less cautious than my friends' instructors, and allowed me to go probably sooner than I need have done.

I suppose most pilots remember their first solo. I certainly remember mine.

I had been up with my instructor for about half an hour one afternoon, when he said to me: "Do you think you can take her round yourself now? Do you know the country well enough not to get lost?"

I assured him I was O.K. and quite confident... more so than I actually felt; and we landed. He climbed out of the front cockpit, made secure the straps, and waved me off.

As I taxied into wind I was very conscious of the empty cockpit in front of me, but I would not have had anyone in it for anything.

As soon as I opened the throttles fully and we moved forward with the tail off the ground, I felt perfectly confident. Up she came, and away went the hangars below. I was alone, alone for the first time in my life in the air, and I was happy. It was marvellous.

I flew abominably, I know - forgetting all the finer points I had been taught - but I did not care. There was no one to watch me or tick me off. I was alone, and in control - or thought I was. This was something worth living for, worth working for.

I enjoyed every moment of it. I loved the feel of the cold, clean wind on my face, tearing at my goggles and trying to lift my helmet off my head; I enjoyed the movement as I banked, with the ground appearing to tilt as I leaned over... the horizon coming above my head on one side and disappearing below me on the other; I enjoyed the lift or drop of the aeroplane as we bumped in an air pocket, but most of all I thrilled with the feel of power. I was in control. I could go where I wished. I could stay up, or I could land... at any rate, I hoped I could!

I flew around, sometimes looking at the ground, glancing at my instruments, or gazing about me. Yes, I was happy... very happy.

I approached to land... realized I was too fast, so eased the stick back slightly. We were over the aerodrome, and still fifty feet from the ground. I pushed the stick gently forward, hoping she would make it, but the speed became too high again.

Back on the stick once more, and it was obvious I should not make it this time. The hangars were coming uncomfortably close, and I was travelling far too fast to touch down. I opened the throttle fully.

I made a wider circuit this time, looking at the wind-sock as I went round, to make certain the wind had not changed, started gliding from further off, and this time made a reasonable landing.

Before we passed out we had to take a final test. I was tested by the Wing Commander, whom I liked the look of very much. This was the first time I had met him, and I think he knew how nervous I was feeling.

We climbed in, and he said to me: "Go through your cockpit drill, then taxi out, climb to four thousand feet, and I'll tell you what to do next."

One of the ground crew was standing by to swing the prop., so I called out: "Switches off, petrol on, throttles closed."

"No, they're not, they're on," the Wing Commander quietly said down the speaking tube.

What a B.F. I felt! I had knocked the switches on when climbing in.

I must do better than this, I said to myself, as I thought of my cockpit drill.

Having completed the drill, I taxied round the perimeter to the take-off point, being very careful to look about me in the approved manner!

I was pleased with my take-off, as I knew it was a good one. I got the tail up quickly, kept her perfectly straight, and rose without bumping.

I had taken the precaution of setting the wind direction on my compass before I took off, *310*, so was able to check my course and direction quite easily. It would also be a check when landing into wind.

I climbed to four thousand feet as directed. It was very bumpy below two thousand feet, but became quite smooth above that height.

The first thing I had to do when we were up there was a number of 360 degree turns: it meant turning in a complete circle and straightening out on to my original course. I had no gyro compass, so I had to pick a point on the ground. There was an aerodrome below on my right, so I had only to keep turning and level out as it came round again. I did one of these to either side, and was next told to do the same thing as steeply as possible.

This was not quite so simple. However, there was a good horizon, and I think I did quite reasonable turns. I had noted my height, which remained constant the whole time: this showed that I was turning without dropping or lifting the aeroplane's nose. Again the aerodrome was very useful, as I was able to straighten her out pretty well dead on course.

"I'm going to put her into a spin, and when I say 'right,' I want you to pull her out."

The Wing Commander closed the throttle, and I watched the air speed drop... *75... 70... 65... 58... 55... 50...*

Stalling... Down went the nose, and round she went.

I watched the ground spinning round, and then

"*Right!*"

I kicked hard on the left rudder, centralized the stick, waited until the ground appeared still, and centralized the rudder; then raised the nose by pulling back the stick and opening the throttle.

"That was good," I heard.

I was really enjoying myself, and wished I could stay up for hours, tumbling and gliding about the sky.

"D'you know where the aerodrome is?" I heard again.

"Yes, sir."

"Set course for there, then."

I turned in the direction I hoped the aerodrome was, and apparently guessed right, as I was not corrected. I was then told to do a 360 degree gliding turn, first to the left, and then straightway to the right.

I allowed my air speed to build up a bit too much while doing this, which meant we lost more height than was necessary. Next a steep gliding turn... then some side-slipping, and so back to the aerodrome and what I considered the most difficult part of the test, landing.

There was a factory chimney quite close, and I watched the smoke very carefully to get the exact wind direction. *Blast those bumps!* She was being chucked about all over the place, and I had to keep correcting her instead of settling down to a comfortable glide and concentrating on my air speed and approach.

We were over the aerodrome... *fifty feet... twenty feet...* I eased back the stick, the air speed dropped, then... *Bump!* Blast, I had duffed it!

I opened the throttle fully, and started to climb again.

"Why did you do that?" the Wing Commander asked. "Your landing was all right. You needn't have taken off again."

I suppose I had been expecting to make a bad landing, and as soon as I felt the wheels touch the ground I imagined I was going to bounce, and so took off again. (By the way, we were taught that unless we made a good landing we should take off again immediately, rather than let the aircraft go on bouncing.)

The second time I did bounce, but I let her stay down as I imagined I was *not* going to! However, much to my delight and relief, the Wing Commander said I had done reasonably well.

And now I am on leave; waiting...

I have done a lot of waiting during the last three years, and it has always been worth while. I started off by waiting: I wanted to join the R.A.F. right at the beginning of the war, but this was not to be. I had to wait. I was very impatient, too: I was even worried lest the war be over before I started!

I had my interview and medical in November 1939, and was told I should hear the results shortly. A week later I was told that my eyesight was not up to the standard necessary for air crew.

I wrote protesting, saying I could see to shoot perfectly well, played most games, and in fact had excellent eyesight! Later I heard that my case had been reconsidered, and I was fully up to the required medical standard, but that as I was in a reserved occupation, my application could not be considered.

I replied that I was not being called up, but was volunteering with the knowledge and full approval of my employers. I was then informed that if I could produce satisfactory proof that they were willing to release me for the duration, my application would be reconsidered. I next had to go to my employers saying I was called up, and so was able to supply the necessary information; and at long last I was in.

Somehow the last four years seem all that really matter... yet I am the same. I would not have believed so much could have happened, and still remain unaltered... yet I don't see why, not. My likes and dislikes have not changed, but I don't think the same small things affect or worry me to the extent they used to do. I think I am more tolerant, and less critical.

After I had been rescued from a dinghy in the North Sea nearly two years ago, I said to a friend: "I can't tell you how good it is to be alive. I feel as though I shall never again mind what happens. I shall never be worried by petty woes: I shall never be unhappy, or grumble. I shall always be content."

"You are wrong," my friend replied. "In a month you will feel differently; you will feel as you used to do."

And my friend was right: I do feel as I have always done... or nearly so.

One evening, when I had just started my training as an air gunner, an order came through that all gunners were to stand by the aeroplanes with parachutes and full flying kit immediately. We did not know the reason... whether there was some emergency really on, or if it was merely a precautionary measure. We guessed, and hoped, that there might be possibly a U-boat sighted somewhere off the coast, and we would be sent out to attack it.

I rushed out with the others to an aeroplane, although I had never even flown, hoping to nip in unobserved!

After we had been aboard for some minutes, we were ordered back, full of disappointment, to our quarters. If we had had to go out, I should have been useless, but I did not think of that then, or care either, for that matter. I hoped I should see some action... some fun: I wanted to get going straight away. I was impatient and very ignorant.

Before I started operating I was careless as to whether I got through or not. I knew I was in for a dangerous job, but this did not worry me. I was very ignorant! People used to say - '*Oh... so you're going to be a tail gunner.*' as much as to say - '*You won't last long.*' - but I did not mind: I only laughed. I was ignorant... very ignorant!

I thought, if I went... I went, and that would be that. It meant nothing to me; I did not understand. I never contemplated what might happen to me; I do not think it seriously entered my head. I did not know what it would be like to be amongst exploding shells... to have bullets aimed and fired at me, or to feel afraid. I joined the R.A.F. to fight. I wanted to fight, and I did not know what it would be like.

But now I know!

If I had known before, would I have been an air gunner? The answer is *yes*... definitely *yes*.

Not that I am a brave man... very far from it.

There is a wonderful sense of satisfaction in completing a bombing raid. If it has been a success, if you know you have found and hit your target, you feel you have accomplished something, and deserve a pat on the back. You may feel very tired when you return from a raid, but if it has been a success you always feel happy and content, and to feel content you must have done something worth while or have satisfied some craving within you.

You set out on a trip prepared... prepared mentally and physically. You provide yourself with all the knowledge and skill you can acquire. Every possible emergency has to be considered and contended with: every possible move or action thought out. You cannot afford to be ignorant, or careless: you cannot afford to be callous, either, for if you are, you are liable to lose that continuous alertness so essential in the air.

Flying should be instinctive, like reading, or riding a bicycle. When you read a book, you do not need to spell out the words, but you recognize them at a glance and without effort. So with flying. Your actions have to become mechanical, and independent of, and even quicker than, your thoughts.

When a pilot first learns to fly, he has to concentrate very hard on all he does, and he gets tired. He has to think, for instance, how much rudder to use in conjunction with ailerons when turning; he has continually to correct his course and air speeds, and to do so is often a mental effort. He gets tired flying on a straight course, but he has to go on until this strain ceases: until he can fly without realizing he is flying.

Then, and not until then, will he be able to look about him in the air without the aeroplane wandering off course: his mind can then be freed from the action of his hands and feet, and he won't get tired from the effort of flying. His brain will be freed and ready, not for the method of his flying but for the purpose of his flying.

When I look back on the pilots I have known and flown with, I know I have an example and a standard before me. When I think of pilots like *Leonard*, *Jimmy*, *Rob by*, *Wilkie*, *Cres*, *Bomber*, *Willie*, and countless others, I know I have something to aim at, something to work for. It is going to be hard work, but it will be worth it. It is what I am now waiting for, but it will be worth the waiting.

Part Two

Part Two

Chapter VII

After a long leave - the longest I have ever had - I received a signal from the Air Ministry instructing me to report at on March 17th. I arrived punctually at nine a.m., as ordered, and spent the remainder of the day in the necessary formalities preparatory for sailing.

I was posted to Canada. This was no surprise, as I had already requested to go there: my chief reason being that I had relations there, and hoped to see them again. Obviously on this occasion Lockie would not be able to accompany me, but I had left her in good hands.

We were supposed to have various inoculations, but I refused, as the last time I was done I felt so confoundedly ill, and I had no intention of feeling the same way on the eve of sailing, and possibly on the voyage when I should probably be feeling ill anyway. You cannot just say you do not want to be inoculated, and leave it at that: oh, no! you must sign a form in red ink to that effect, and this appears on your permanent records and is brought up periodically as a reminder, and a jibe, as it were, at your cowardice.

Our train was due to leave at four o'clock the following morning, so I took the opportunity for a few hours' sleep beforehand, and kipped down in the mess: bottom on one chair, feet on another, newspaper over head.

Much to my annoyance, I was awakened about midnight by an over-conscientious orderly officer saying *Did I mind sitting up, as the C O. was coming in in a few minutes?*

I did mind very much, and felt convinced the C.O. would not, so went off to sleep again, this time undisturbed until an early breakfast at three a.m.

I felt very concerned about our heavy luggage - particularly *my* heavy luggage - as I noticed when we boarded the bus to take us to the station that it had not been moved, and lay where it had been all day, apparently forgotten. This worried me quite a lot, particularly as I had been told earlier in the day that it would be going on in advance.

However, when I made fresh enquiries and showed considerable anxiety, the reply I got was: "Don't worry; you'll see it again when you arrive. Everybody always worries about their luggage, but it never gets lost!"

I could only hope that ours would not prove an exception.

At the port of embarkation I again made enquiries, and received a similar reply. In spite of everyone's assuring manner, I should have felt very much happier if I could have seen it.

Naturally there was a lot of speculation as to what ship we should be sailing by. I think we all hoped that it would be by a large, fast ship, rather than by a slower convoy. Our hopes were realized, as we soon found ourselves aboard one of our luxury liners. She was far from being a luxury liner, though, when we saw her lying at anchor, painted grey, and heavily armed. She resembled more a mighty man-o'-war than the peaceful vessel for which she was originally intended.

The cabin to which I was allotted had been, I imagine, in earlier days a state room; but with twenty-four bunks in tiers of three it resembled more the interior of some barrack block.

I do not quite know what I had visualized the voyage might be like: probably very comfortable, and possibly exciting. Actually it was neither. We were on a troopship with the rigid discipline of such. We were not there to be comfortable, but were merely a valuable cargo to be transferred across the Atlantic as quickly as possible; and it was the job of those in command to see that the trip was *not* exciting.

The food was certainly marvellous - apparently unrationed - and for the next few days I made a pig of myself at every meal, eating large quantities of sugar, butter, eggs, and white bread. I think the white bread was the greatest treat.

As I was eating my first meal I thought of the people on shore, only a mile away, still eating war meal bread with a scraping of butter, and drinking half-sweetened tea or coffee. Probably they were enjoying it, as I had done, saying how simple it really was to make do with the rations, and how lucky they were: *think of the rations the Germans had!*

I was under no illusions at all. I realized what a lucky chap I was. I was doing exactly what I had wanted to do: I was learning to fly; I was travelling; I was eating all the food I wanted; I was leaving the blackout behind. I think probably, in imagination, this is what appealed to me more than anything else… to see lighted cities again; bright neon signs; shop windows gay and inviting; and all the other allurements of a city's night life.

We did not sail until the following evening, as more people were continually arriving on board. There was nothing to do but walk up and down, and talk, and wait for the next meal.

I talked for some time with a P.R.U. pilot, and learnt something about his work, about which I had previously had quite the wrong conception.

A young Dutchman, Eric, also starting his training as a pilot, had the bunk next to mine and the place next to me in the dining saloon. I asked him how long he had been in England, and how he got over.

His first attempt to escape had been unsuccessful, but he eventually arrived in the late autumn of 1940.

I also asked him what the Dutch people thought of the Germans. He said they started by hating them, but now they despised them.

I made still further enquiries about my luggage before we sailed, as I was beginning to feel really anxious about it. I could see tender upon tender arriving alongside the ship, and looked down at net-loads of trunks, cases and kitbags, all looking exactly like mine, being hauled up and deposited in the interior of our monstrous ship. I went down to the hold, and felt like a dwarf among the piles of thousands of kitbags and cabin trunks stacked high upon each other. I could only hope that my things were not amongst those at the bottom!

Tugs, tenders and launches were fussing around the ship all day: delivering people, luggage, mail, food; taking off naval officers, and civilians with important-looking brief cases. The scene lacked the excitement and flurry of peacetime ocean sailings: there was no one to see us off, no friends to say good-bye, no hand waves and brightly coloured dresses.

The atmosphere was one of secrecy, and quiet efficiency. The time we would leave was a secret: our final destination was a secret.

Almost every branch of the service was represented among the passengers: R.A.F., Navy, Army, Fleet Air Arm, Merchant Navy, Marines, some civilians, and also there was a batch of survivors from a torpedoed ship. There were British, American, Dutch, French, Poles, Norwegians, Czechs. Some were returning to their own country; some were making a routine journey; others were crossing the Atlantic for the first time.

I went to sleep that night trying not to hear the babble of different tongues in my cabin. A Belgian and a Czech were conversing in English; Poles, Czechs and Dutchmen were chattering in their own languages; and in the next cabin I could hear Canadians and Americans arguing.

I learnt to admire the Poles on that journey. I saw a lot of them, and talked to many of them.

It seems incredible that anyone could endure the hardships they have been through and still remain cheerful or even sane. No one, without having the highest courage, endurance, and outstanding character, could possibly have surmounted the innumerable hardships and difficulties to enable them to reach England as they have done. This undoubtedly accounts for the magnificent type of the majority of the Poles over here.

I was told of one who had refused an important and highly paid technical job at the Admiralty in order that he might join the R.A.F. to fight and avenge. That is their one object... *revenge*, and I think the thought of it has enabled them to endure so much. After all, it is the only thing many of them have left to live for.

I have never heard them complain of their past hardships, though God knows they have enough grounds for complaint. Many of them are men of high culture and old families: many of them came here speaking little or no English, and without friends. They do not ask for, or expect sympathy; all they want is a chance to fight... *revenge*. They have lost their homes; many have seen their families tortured and massacred; some of them have held senior ranks in the Polish Army or Air Force, and are now of very junior rank in England, but still they do not complain. So long as they are able to get revenge, they are content.

There was one Pole in our cabin whose name was Tony. He was a small, sturdily built man of twenty-two, but looked nearer thirty. He had a long scar down one side of his face, and was nearly always smiling. There were times, though, when there was no smile, and his face had a terribly sad look: a look of yearning after something lost, or of seeing far back into the past, a look of utter misery and dismay. I have noticed the same expression on the faces of other Poles.

If you speak to Tony, a beaming smile will brighten his face, and he will come towards you saying: "Ah, my friend... you are my friend." He is pathetically grateful for any friendship. I asked him once if he knew a certain English R.A.F. officer, and he replied: "I love him... he is my very good friend." Tony loved the girls, and frequently appealed to me for suitable endearments when writing to his old flames!

Tony spent two years in a German prison camp, and suffered almost daily beatings: all his ribs have been broken, and his body is a mass of scars. But to see Tony, with his smile and laughing eyes, you might think his life had been spent in gaiety and fun.

Tony is only one of many. He is here by his courage and endurance, and it will be a bad day for the Nazis when he and those like him get their revenge.

I cannot say I enjoyed that voyage very much. The ship was crowded; I had no intimate friends with me; and there were too many people aboard for the usual'board-ship friendships to spring up. One can feel more lonely in a crowd than when one is completely alone.

When I felt particularly depressed or lonely I thought of Tony, and wondered what right had I - with practically everything I needed, doing exactly what I wanted, going where I chose - to be anything but content?

At our table in the dining room there were two Coastal Command pilots, a Canadian navigator, an American Ferry Command navigator, Eric, the Dutch u/t pilot I have previously mentioned, and myself. The

Coastal Command pilots spent most of their time at meals remarking how glad they were to be in Coastal Command; how much more versatile they had to be than Bomber Command pilots; how far superior and more accurate their navigation had to be; how much more varied was their job compared with Bomber Command's; how many more flying hours they had to put in; how much more difficult to find and hit were their targets; how far fouler weather they had to fly through, and so on. One of them remarked to me that Bomber Command personnel did not often visit Coastal Command aerodromes!

I replied - "No, not if we could help it!" So we carried on, like schoolboys cracking up the merits of their respective schools.

There is always rivalry - 'professional jealousy' I suppose you might call it - between Commands; yet how well they co-operate when the necessity arises. I am eternally grateful to Coastal Command, as they once spotted our dinghy afloat in the North Sea when we had about given up hope of being rescued, but I did not tell my table companions this!

The American told us repeatedly that if the voyage lasted much longer and he was kept out of the air many more days, we should lose the war.

I was intrigued with a poker game that went on, as far as I could see, practically non-stop throughout the voyage. The players were all Americans, who seemed oblivious of the crowds gathered permanently around their table, watching them. Whenever I passed, the game was always in progress, and the crowd, silent and intent, always watching.

I had heard of the round-the-clock poker game, but had never before seen one in progress.

The players sat round their table in shirt-sleeves, with neck-ties loosened and with hats tilted to the backs of their heads, apparently indifferent as to whether the game continued or if they lost or won. I had the feeling that whatever outer clothing might be discarded, the hats would always remain tilted on the backs of their heads.

I was struck with the extreme caution and suspicion with which the game was played. When each player had been dealt his five cards, he would carefully slide them along the table; stack them neatly together; cautiously pick them up; cup them in his hands so that there was no possible chance of the cards being seen by anyone else; move the corners just far enough apart to take a rapid glance at their values; remove the unwanted cards, and then replace them face downwards on the table.

The discarded cards would then be returned to the dealer, who would give the necessary numbers in return. These would be collected and shuffled carefully with the remainder of the original five cards, before being looked at; the whole proceeding denoting the utmost caution, suspicion, indifference, and even boredom.

One player, I noticed, having gone through the usual rigmarole of shuffling his cards, returned them unlooked at to the table, and bringing a penknife out of his pocket, began to pare and clean his nails. The others took not the slightest notice or showed any signs of surprise or impatience, but rather seemed to look upon the proceeding as a legitimate, if not necessary, part of the game.

I mentioned this to a poker-playing friend, and he explained that it would have been definitely part of the game. If the player had been playing for really high stakes, which he was, the others would have noticed any change in his expression or manner, and possibly would have gained some clue as to the value of his hand. The diversion was necessary to compose his manner.

Our American table companion was among the players, and I enquired how he was doing. He was about five hundred dollars to the good, but it might have been five hundred tiddly winks for all the emotion or pleasure he showed. 1 wondered if there was pleasure in the game, if you could call it such: certainly there was no indication of it evident in the demeanour of the performers. The strain, I should imagine, must have been terrific, and I wondered if it was worth it.

Two of the players were from our 'survivor' passengers. Possibly they had been playing a similar game when their ship had been torpedoed. I had the impression that nothing short of a torpedo would break up the game I was watching!

The sea was rough for a couple of days, and a voice kept blaring through loud speakers distributed about the ship - "Give up but don't give in!"

A man in our cabin had lain prostrate, completely under the weather during this rough period. In the middle of the second day he could stand the voice no longer and sat up in his bunk shouting at the top of his voice, "Silly bloody… ; he's never been seasick in his life!"

Chapter VIII

We arrived at - early one morning, and disembarked at about eight a.m. straight on to a special train waiting to take us to -. I made still further enquiries about our luggage, which I was beginning to feel I should never see again, yet everyone but me seemed confident of its safety.

Most people rushed to buy a paper as soon as we got ashore. I was immediately struck by the size of the newspaper; very different from our war-time editions, yet I could not find any more news.

The headlines greeting me were - 'SIX DIE IN PLANE CRASH' - a tragedy in itself, but of national importance…? It made me realize how far away I was from the war.

In Canada, three thousand miles from the fighting, the individual counted; was of importance as an individual. When he died, provided he did not die in his own bed, he was news. In war the individual ceases to count: he is part of a machine; a vast, organized scheme. He is trained to work to a plan. If he dies, his friends and family will suffer: he will be a loss to the nation not as an individual but as a number, and he will have to be replaced; but he will not be the subject of newspaper headlines. Yet whether his death is proclaimed simultaneously to thousands of people, or whether a grieving wife or mother will get the dreaded official telegram, his death will be a tragedy to those who knew him, but a tragedy taking its place in the world about him.

I had rather imagined that when I camp to Canada I should be about the only person in R.A.F. uniform. I certainly did not think that I should see nearly as many uniforms about the cities and towns of Canada as one sees in England, but such was the case. Whenever our train stopped on its way to , which was often, I saw people in uniform - mostly Army - and the conductor of the train told me that in one village we stopped at there was not one man left of military age.

The Canadians are proud of their men-folk who are fighting, and I think this partly explains the headlines that so surprised me at first glance. The six men who died in the plane crash were airmen under training. They had lost their lives on active service: they were men learning to fight for their country. The news of their death was made public not so much as some dramatic incident, but rather as a gesture or reminder that Canada was in the war... was sacrificing the life blood of her young men; was united with England in a mutual purpose. It was something that the average reader could grasp probably far more than that the Ruhr or Berlin had had so many more tons of bombs unloaded the previous night, or that a South Coast town in England had been bombed.

Whenever we stopped at a station people seemed very friendly. At one town, Truro, women were walking the length of the train with basket-loads of lovely red apples. At first we felt disappointed, thinking they were for sale - as we had no Canadian money with us - but they were pressed on us as gifts, and very welcome they were, too! I felt it was a happy omen, and a delightfully simple welcome to a strange country. I heard afterwards that no matter what times the trains, with fresh arrivals from England, stopped there, those women were always waiting with their basket-loads of apples.

The Poles in our party were thrilled with the journey: they said the scenery was like Poland and parts of Russia. The Czechs said it was like their country. The Dutch claimed parts as being like Holland. I thought the parts we were going through were like the less beautiful portions of Scotland; parts like Hampshire or Wiltshire on a large scale, and parts like an enlarged and untidy Essex or Lincolnshire.

We none of us had any Canadian money, and only a limited supply of small change in English money, as ours had been taken from us on the ship. I saw several people give two-shilling-pieces and half-crowns for newspapers or ten-cent magazines. It is extraordinary how, when one has been prevented from shopping for some days, any chance to buy is irresistible.

We arrived at that evening.

That first evening with no black-out was a real treat and quite a thrill, and something to which I had been really looking forward. I found myself wandering about in the night, just for the sake of seeing lights and unshuttered windows. At times I felt rather ashamed that I was so safe and so far away from the war... at any rate ashamed of being glad that I was away for a bit.

I had not realized what a strain one lived in a great deal of the time at home: subconsciously alert, waiting for something the whole time.

During the evening all the lights suddenly went out in the mess. My first and instinctive reaction was '*Air Raid!*' and automatically I was ready to take any necessary precautions. I found myself listening for the drone of aeroplanes overhead.

Obviously I realized almost instantly where I was, and was amazed how one's nerves automatically react to the suggestion of bombs, although no such danger could possibly exist. I often had the same instinctive reaction for the first few days when I heard a train whistle, which sounds very like the opening blasts of our air raid siren.

I remember in 1941, when our aerodrome used to get bombed fairly regularly, any noise in the least resembling a siren made us ready immediately to take action. Cars revving up to change gear were particularly trying at times. Anyone who banged a door was most unpopular, and the humourist who whistled like a bomb was a positive menace!

Those who have been bombed regularly will probably sympathize. Any noise that even suggests an approaching air raid and the falling of bombs immediately makes one more alert: one listens for approaching aeroplanes, that tell-tale irregular throb; for the descending whistling note of a falling bomb. One is ready, and if the necessity arises goes flat on the floor, under a table or bed, without realizing or remembering how one got there.

One evening at my old squadron I was brushing my teeth just before getting into bed, when I heard an aeroplane approaching fast and low. I was under the bed when the bombs burst less than a hundred yards away. I do not remember getting there, but when I got up from my hiding place I still had the tooth brush in my mouth. There was nothing to tell me it was not one of our own aircraft as the sirens had not sounded… only instinct.

On another occasion I was with a navigator friend in the mess, with all the lights out. We were the only occupants of the ante-room - everyone else being outside or in a shelter - and we were listening to a Jerry circling overhead. We had been down the shelter at about the same time every night for the past week or more, and the mess was still intact, so we decided to stay where we were.

My navigator friend began giving a commentary of an imaginary bombing run-up: "Bomb doors open. Bombs fused. Steady… left… left… steady. Left… steady. Hold it!… Bombs gone!"

As he said 'Bombs gone,' the unearthly whistling started. I thought he was being a bit too realistic and carrying his commentary too far, when the mess shook and plaster fell on us from the ceiling as a stick of bombs fell just outside!

I waited five days at -, which is a vast disposal centre for those arriving in Canada and for those about to embark for the United Kingdom. I was waiting for posting to an E.F.T.S.

I was eventually posted to De Winton, in Alberta, about three thousand miles away, and the idea of a four days' train journey did not appeal very much. Nevertheless, when the time came I definitely enjoyed it.

One talks of England as the 'Old Country,' but my impression while travelling across Canada was that I was in an old country then… very old and very tired, with its miles upon miles of forests of fir trees interspersed with silver birches; its gigantic lakes, huge rushing rocky rivers, and vast expanses of nothingness. Yes, I thought Canada seemed very old, wild… in some parts untamable and with many secrets. It seemed to stare at you, unwinking, keeping its secrets hidden; toughened by the weather; forbidding to strangers; asking no sympathy and giving none: but still with a fierce gigantic beauty… a beauty not dependent on colour - indeed almost rejecting colour as frivolous - but a beauty of size and space, independent of man.

It is so unlike England, where man has, if anything, enhanced the beauty by a network of countless hedges; by villages, churches, avenues, park lands and farms. The beauty of England is intimate and friendly: it welcomes you; invites you to stay, look longer, and be comforted.

We had a few hours in Montreal.

I thought Montreal a very beautiful city. Whether it was the contrast from the flat, desolate, and rather depressing country we had passed through during the previous few hours, or whether the city really was as beautiful as I imagined, I do not know. However, I passed a happy two hours wandering around, gazing into shop windows and sauntering through the stores, beautifully decorated and lit by hundreds of lights. I was still awe-inspired by so much light, such full shops, and so much to buy.

I felt terribly sorry for the airmen on that journey: they were crowded into uncomfortable coaches, where they lived, ate and slept… the seats being converted into bunks at night. They were incredibly cheerful, though, despite what seemed to me beastly discomfort.

Many of them looked a bit bewildered. Probably this was the first time some of them had been away from home, at any rate so far away. I wondered if they fully realized what they were doing? Probably not. They might take it as a matter of course, or as an adventure.

They had all been in the Air Force for some months, and were more or less used to being pushed around with the usual alternations of sweat and nothing to do. Probably this journey would be looked upon merely as another move, mingled with novelty and the possibility of excitement.

I used to look at those strange faces - not knowing any of them, but rather wishing I did - little realizing that one of them was to become one of my greatest friends.

Those lads spent the day sitting in pairs; two pairs facing each other across a table. Some played cards; others read, or talked, or slept. At meal times, a party was detailed to bring food round to the others.

The officers lived in luxury by comparison. There were only about a dozen of us, and we had a coach to ourselves, as well as the use of the dining coach.

I was nothing like as bored with that journey as I thought I should be. The idea of four days and nights in the train sounded horrible, but when the time came, it was not at all bad.

It was interesting and amusing, comparing the trains and travelling with our own trains and train journeys.

There was far more use of the steam whistle than one hears in England. Over every level crossing, none of which have gates - the bigger ones having a bell and an arm that swings backwards and forwards when a train is approaching - the whistle bellows the morse symbol for *Q*: *dar-dar-di-dar*. It seems to wail it out in an urgent, almost heartrending appeal for everyone to take note, not only as a herald of so much might and importance passing, but also as a warning cry to anybody or anything foolish enough to be in its path.

I spent part of the time in the back of the train, in the conductor's caboose - in a glass-sided box perched up above the level of the carriages. I sat swaying, jolted from side to side by the movement of the train, watching the view and listening to the reminiscences of the conductors. Each conductor travels the length of his own stretch of line, and then hands over to the next man.

They gave me the history of the track, with stories of its laying, which some of them had witnessed. Each man knew his own stretch intimately, and pointed with pride to landmarks of singular interest. One man was particularly keen on fishing, and gave me the weight, size, shape and colour of the fish to be caught in every stretch of water we saw.

Some of them had been in England in the last war, and were as interested to hear about the 'Old Country,' as I was about the 'New.'

Whenever we stopped at a station - or to take on water or coals, or at a loop line to let another train pass - we used to get out and stretch our legs, and those who had any money, to buy apples, oranges or papers… until the cry: *All aboard!* sent us back to the train.

At night, a negro sleeping car porter made our beds, talking continuously to himself and all and sundry: "*Git down dar, pillow! Stay where ah puts yo. Where is yo now?*"

The following day we passed through hundreds of miles of unbroken forest of fir trees, with here and there silver birches trying to make their graceful, slender, scintillating trunks seen through the thick confusion of cumbrous dark foliage of the fir trees endeavouring to swamp them. The train wound its way, twisting and turning through this seemingly endless forest as though seeking an escape.

Here and there in a clearing we could see small lakes covered with ice and snow. Occasionally a trapper would shuffle on his snow boots, slowly across one of these lakes. He, or possibly an elk or timber wolf, would be the only signs of life: the country, like so many of its animals, seemed to hibernate throughout the winter. There was practically no variety of colour: dark greens and browns; greys and white; yet without doubt the whole was a scene of beauty... beauty on a large scale, a grand, fierce, sleeping beauty. On a large lake we saw the wooden huts built by the fishermen for their winter's toil.

Then, suddenly, in the early afternoon we came upon Lake Superior; and from then until dark, we passed through some of the most beautiful country I have ever seen. I have driven through lovely country for a few hours on end, but never before without a break for half a day.

For the most part the train ran alongside the lake, twisting and turning about, and only occasionally losing sight of the water. It was all on such a vast scale that it was only possible to take in a small part at once. I tried taking photographs, but again only such a small part of so much hugeness could be seen.

We passed through two German prison camps. I should imagine from the treatment, the amount of food, and the beauty of the surroundings, many of the prisoners will be jolly sorry when the war is over. The train conductor told me with some disgust that they are even given beer!

We arrived at Winnipeg at about eight-thirty the following morning, where there was a reception to welcome us at the station. Several people nearly missed this reception, owing to the early hour, but I think everyone had a look in, even if for only a few minutes.

I had heard something of the hospitality of Winnipeg, and what I had heard certainly showed itself that morning. We were ushered into the large central hall of the station, where there was a band, many people with handshakes, pretty girls, refreshments, and much kindness. I felt that if our arrival had been at eight-thirty p.m. instead of at eight-thirty a.m., we should have appreciated and enjoyed our welcome even more. As it was, three of our party successfully managed to get left behind, and at least a dozen very nearly got left behind, and would have done so if the train had not obligingly stopped just outside the station!

All that day we were in the prairies.

There is very little variety in the enormous expanse of the Canadian prairie, except that possibly parts are more monotonous than others. All day we went through the flat, uninteresting country, with its rectangular fields dotted here and there with farms, and each farm with its wooden house and small metal windmill. To make the scene even more dreary, the snow was melting, and the fields that were not covered with snow were partly - and sometimes entirely - submerged with water. Possibly a first sight of the prairies in the autumn might be impressive or even beautiful, but in the early spring there could be no claim to either. I must say after I had lived on the prairies for a bit, my first impression altered considerably; and those who know them really well find them beautiful.

What a contrast with the previous afternoon! I looked out on the landscape, with its horizon, in parts, as flat as the sea, and for the first time during that journey across Canada I felt depressed.

The following morning we awoke within sight of the Rockies.

The name alone... *Rocky Mountains*, suggests something great; something grand and majestic. They were well over a hundred miles away when I first saw them... a long line of jagged peaks, somehow unexpected beyond the flat prairie. I had no eyes then for the desertlike country through which we were passing, but could only watch the fascinating vision in the distance.

The sun tinted the mountains a wonderful coral pink, which gradually got lighter... became bluer, and then a dazzling white: almost like some romantic stage setting. I watched them and marvelled as they changed colour: they seemed always to be changing colour. Whenever I looked at the Rockies - which was often - they were always a different colour, and almost seemed to be a different shape sometimes.

We arrived at at seven-fifteen that morning, dead on time and almost exactly eighty-four hours after leaving -. As we pulled into the station we saw a 'cowboy' in traditional western garb. The sight was a novelty which we soon got used to, but I think most people were disappointed he was not packing a brace of guns!

But the sight that pleased me most a few minutes later was my luggage being unloaded from the baggage car. I thought of the Englishman and his proverbial luggage. I seemed to be living up to that reputation, with my large tin trunk, four kit bags, golf club, tennis racquet, squash racquet, not to mention smaller suitcases and surplus coats.

One of the first people I saw in the mess when I got to the aerodrome was the C.O. I noticed he was wearing a Czech wing, as well as his R.A.F. wings.

After being with Czechs, Poles, Dutch and Belgians for so long, and talking very carefully and slowly, I started off: "How - do - you - do? I - have - just - arrived. I - have - had - a - very - long - journey."

I think he thought I was drunk!

Chapter IX

We did not waste any time, but started flying the following day.

I was introduced to my instructor, Len Cogan, who started off by saying: "Well, I don't suppose you will be sick, anyway."

I promised him I would not be sick, although at times he did his best to make me!

Len taught me the rudiments of flying, and taught them very well. He never wasted time in the air: each hour we spent together up there was time well spent; an hour nearer to me learning to fly, and an hour's worth of more knowledge of flying.

Len is very fair, small, and quiet, and I have rarely known a man to say less. If you speak to him, he will look at you with large eyes; he will have a humorous tilt to his mouth, but he probably will not answer. It will not be rudeness on his part, but merely one of his mannerisms… a mannerism you soon get used to, and indeed, expect, and often respect.

He was the same in the air. He never spoke for the sake of talking, but everything he said was of vital importance and had to be remembered. He told me before we set out on our first trip together, that when he taught me anything, he did not want to have to go through that thing again… but if I did not understand what he wanted, he did not mind how many times he showed it to me, provided I told him I did not understand. Usually it was not necessary, but when I did not grasp what he wanted, he was wonderfully patient. Yes, Len was a good instructor, and taught me a lot, and I am very grateful to him.

Before we took to the air on our first trip he showed me the cockpit layout, and the elements of taxi-ing. The *Tiger Moths* we were using were fitted with wheel brakes, which at first took a bit of getting used to, as they were very sensitive with the rudders. When we were in the air, he taught me the proper use of the controls, and the significance of the instruments; he showed me the action in the event of fire, and the correct method of abandoning the aircraft.

I knew on that first trip that I had a good instructor, but I knew it better and appreciated it even more later on. I was lucky... very lucky.

Our first trip lasted an hour, and every minute was of value.

I realize now, far more than I did then, how important is every hour spent in the air, and how necessary it is to use every moment of that hour to its best advantage. The pilot has so much to learn... and when he has learnt it, must forget how he learnt it, and act instinctively - quicker than conscious thought. His mind must be free to think, not of his actions, but of events that dictate those actions: he must learn to fly without thinking of how he is flying; he must have his thoughts free for the many and varied problems surrounding him in his flight.

When he is flying the pilot is also navigator and engineer. He may be carrying in his crew a navigator and a flight engineer, yet the whole time he is checking mentally the navigation of his flight, and watching, and listening subconsciously to, the performance of his engines.

Len used to make me fly using the lightest possible touch on the stick, and with my feet barely resting on the rudder bars. Often, when I used to find myself flying really badly, I found it was due to the fact that I was gripping the stick for all I was worth and had my feet locked firmly to the rudder bar. As soon as I made myself relax, my flying at once improved. By straining my muscles I was tiring myself physically, and not giving the aeroplane a fair chance.

Most aeroplanes will practically fly themselves, if you will only let them; they need only a little encouragement and persuasion to keep straight. The physical energy you use to fly light aeroplanes is negligible, although if you start fighting them it can be really tiring.

Len flew the *Tiger Moth* just about perfectly. His flying of that particular type was all it could and should be.

He never showed off by demonstrating aerobatics unnecessarily, as some instructors like to do: in fact, he never did any aerobatics until he considered I was ready to learn them. I must say he made up for lost time later on! He very rarely flew the aeroplane at all, except to demonstrate, so that I got the full benefit of every moment we were in the air.

On our second trip I practised normal turns, climbing turns, gliding turns, and spins. The latter are compulsory before a pupil may be sent solo, and they have to be practised regularly throughout his training. The idea is not to be able to spin an aeroplane, but to be able to recover from a spin as quickly as possible.

Most aeroplanes can be made to spin very easily by stalling them and then applying rudder in either direction. They will also spin through bad flying, and when you certainly do not want them to! If you do a climbing turn with insufficient airspeed, or use too much rudder when doing a gliding turn, they can also very easily spin. As the pupil is liable to do one of these foolish things in his early training, it is essential he should know how to get himself out of his difficulties.

We concentrated on circuits and landings on our third trip.

Before we took off, Len made me notice very carefully how the horizon and surrounding ground looked from where I was sitting: exactly how it looked… how much I could see, and where it appeared to cut the nose of the aeroplane. I think this is the most useful tip I have ever had for landing successfully.

It is a mistake, and can even be disastrous, to look at the ground directly below you when you are coming in to land. Once you get the habit of looking ahead, you can judge distance not in feet, but in inches.

That is why Len made me take such careful note of my surroundings while we were still on the ground, as to do a good three-point landing, the aeroplane should fly a few inches off the ground with the landing wheels and tail wheel the same distance from it - in fact, in the same attitude as she would be in when standing on the ground. To do a perfect landing, you must gradually and very gently raise the nose of the aeroplane from its gliding attitude, until the tail wheel is the same distance from the ground as the landing wheels, and, provided the speed is correct, she will stall and sink gently down. If the speed is too high, she will balloon up, and trouble starts, and if the speed is too low she will drop like a stone before you are ready, and again trouble starts.

Owing, I think, to this simple tip, I had no trouble with those first few landings. Trouble started later, probably from forgetting the advice I had been given!

I made three good landings - Len did not say they were good, but I knew they were without his telling me - and was sent up for a solo check. This also went off reasonably well, and I went up on my own.

The first landing was all right, and then everything went all wrong. I blamed the wind, which increased in strength very considerably - as it has a habit of doing without any warning in the prairies. Actually, the wind probably had very little to do with it: it was just my bad flying. I was too anxious, and trying too hard, and in consequence tensing my muscles.

After that first landing I took off again, and it took me three-quarters of an hour to get down! Each time I tried, something went wrong and I had to open up and go round again. Either I had too much drift, or I bumped badly and ballooned up, or I overshot, or something else prevented me from getting the aeroplane down on the ground. I think it was on my fifth attempt that I made some sort of a landing, and felt very relieved to be down in one piece!

In the very early stages of flying, if you make several false attempts at landing, you can very soon lose confidence and begin to wonder if you will ever get down. The only thing is to keep absolutely calm, try to remember all you have learnt, and tell yourself it is perfectly simple.

I found Len in the instructors' room. He was waiting for me, and he looked at me with his eyes appearing even larger than usual.

"Not so good," I said to his unspoken question. "I'm afraid I had to go round five times."

"Six," Len said.

"No, five."

"Six!"

"How do you know?"

"I followed you round."

Another instructor laughed. "That's an old trick," he remarked. "Always keep a look around you."

I always did after that!

So we progressed: taking off... landing; taking off... landing; until it became almost easy.

Before we were allowed off the circuit and away from the aerodrome, we had to learn how to make forced landings in case of engine failure, and precautionary landings in case we had to land in a field away from the aerodrome, due to bad weather or shortage of petrol.

Forced landings are practised with a dead engine. When your engine cuts, you immediately put the aeroplane into its best gliding attitude and trim it for such; select a suitable field and glide towards it, then have a systematic cockpit check to try and find the cause of the trouble. Provided there is nothing you can do to restart the engine, you glide in to land. The normal method is to lose height by doing a series of gliding turns on the leeward side of the field... always turning so that you are facing the field. You tend, if anything, to overshoot. In the first place, surplus height can always be lost, whereas it cannot be regained without an engine: also, if you are going to hit anything, it is better to hit the far hedge after landing than the near hedge at flying speed.

The idea of a precautionary landing is - should the weather suddenly close down and leave a cloud base of only a few hundred feet - to be able to land the aeroplane in as small a space as possible. To do this, you approach the field flying with the nose of the plane well up and the speed just above stalling point, using plenty of engine. If the approach is well done, the aeroplane will sink very rapidly with very little forward speed, and once on the ground will come to a standstill in a very short space. This type of landing is not easy to do well, but it is very useful for coming down in a small field.

It is all a question of practice. In fact, it is all practice, and then more practice... every day.

Half our day was spent in flying, and the other half in attending lectures. We used to fly alternate mornings and afternoons.

Morning flying started at six-thirty a.m. and went on until one p.m., and afternoon flying was from one o'clock until eight-thirty. The morning lectures started at eight a.m. and went on until midday, and in the afternoon from two until five-thirty...

Our ground instructors were Canadians, with Canadian methods of instruction which I, for one, found extremely difficult to follow. The technique seemed to be to teach a class by probing the pupils for answers to the instructors' questions. The instructor would ask why such and such a thing would happen, and then anyone who knew - or thought he knew - the answer, would immediately give tongue. As there were usually at least half a dozen different answers given to each question, I found it extremely difficult - unless I happened to know the right answer myself, which was not often - to know what was wanted.

I suppose, taking it all round, navigation was the hardest subject. There was a new scheme out, known as *Mental D.R.*, which we had to learn. As far as I was concerned, there was very little mental work about it, as it was a question of doing ratios, percentages and division in your head... all quite beyond my powers of mental arithmetic.

I looked upon morse as a subject in which anyone who put in a reasonable amount of work should be able to get a hundred per cent mark in his examination. We had morse practice practically every day, and there was no excuse, really, to be anything but perfect at the speed - which was eight words a minute - at which we had to receive. It surprised me, even so, that there were a few who were anything but perfect.

A subject I found really difficult was *Aircraft Recognition*: I always have done. We had sixty-eight aircraft on our syllabus, and they had to be learnt, together with their wing spans, nationalities, and uses. I spent hours looking at slides, pictures, and silhouettes: trying to remember their shapes... how many rudders they had, whether they were high wing or low wing, and so on. There were times when I thought I should never learn them, and felt very depressed about the whole business, but gradually they began to sort themselves out and make sense.

For our examination we had slides of the different aeroplanes projected on to a screen. Each photograph of silhouette was shown for three seconds... then there was a further five seconds in which to write down the aircraft, nationality, use and wing span. It allowed no time for fumbling about.

A few of the slides were cracked, which I found a great help! For instance, if a certain slide had a crack across the top left hand corner, I knew it was a *Fulmar*; or if the crack went across the bottom left hand corner, I knew it was a *Macchi* 202. Not orthodox, maybe... but helpful!

Chapter X

Five of us used to have evening classes amongst ourselves in our rooms, to help each other along. There was Rob, Chris and Eric, who were Dutchman, Pierre, a Belgian... and myself.

Rob was our chief source of information. His English was far from perfect, but he was frightfully keen to learn, and he used to enjoy talking and trying to explain things, to improve his knowledge of the language. He used to translate all his notes, which he took down in English, into Dutch for the benefit of the other Dutchmen on the course.

I used to marvel at those fellows, learning in what was a foreign language to them. It was all I could do to keep abreast of the work in my own language, and how they managed in one which they were learning, I do not know. At least, I do know: it was hard work and guts.

Rob had been in England about six months before he started this course. He had been an officer in the Dutch Cavalry for eight years. Most Dutchmen are very clean and tidy in their appearance, but Rob was even more so. He was big and powerfully built, and, as he put it, - 'loved the girls.' They loved him, too!

Chris and Eric were half-brothers: young, very gay, and apparently irresponsible, but very responsible when the necessity arose. They were absolutely inseparable.

Pierre and I were the old men of the party. It did not matter to Pierre if our discussions were held in English, Dutch, or French, as he could speak all three languages fluently. It mattered to me, though, very much... so we spoke in English!

Pierre had a wonderful sense of humour, and there was a standing joke between us. He could never pronounce an *aitch* first go off, and used to say to me: "'Ow are you, Richard?" I would adopt a very surprised tone: "I beg your pardon, Pierre?" - and he would reply: "How are you, Richard?" The same sort of thing happened whenever he forgot an *aitch*. I must say he improved!

He used to spend all his spare money on presents for his wife: he would not send them home, for fear they should get lost, but kept them in a box in his room. The box was labelled with his wife's name and address, with instructions that it was to be sent off to her should anything happen to him.

I am pleased to say that I met Pierre and his wife some months later, in London.

It was not long before we received a rude shock: by no means all of us would finish the course. The standard required was very high, and we could be thrown off for failing in ground subjects, as well as for failing to reach the necessary standard in the air. We had to pass in all ground subjects with a minimum total of sixty per cent, as well as in all our air tests.

It was depressing, watching people rejected. Although early on there were comparatively few, the numbers greatly increased when we got to S.F.T.S. I will say that I think, if anything, it made us work harder, and showed us that it was to be no easy job.

There is no doubt that pilots' courses are becoming increasingly stiffer, particularly in ground work. A year before I started my course, it was unusual for anyone to fail. Certainly the same thing cannot be said now.

After our final ground exams I felt a bit dubious about my navigation result, and went for a preview while the papers were being marked. Mine had just been finished, and I received a horrible scare when I heard I had failed by two marks. About half an hour later I was wandering about feeling utterly dejected and miserable, when our instructor came and told me he had found a question he had overlooked to mark!

A very important, and I personally think very interesting part of our training, was in instrument flying. The main flying instruments consist of compass, gyro-direction indicator, artificial horizon, turn and bank and side-slip indicator, rate of climb and descent indicator, altimeter and air speed indicator. When we practised instrument flying, we had to draw a hood over the cockpit, so that only the instruments could be seen... nothing outside. It was a curious sensation at first, being 'under the hood,' in darkness, seeing nothing but a few luminated dials, the only indication as to what the aeroplane was doing.

The hardest part first off was to believe the instruments, and not to go by feel. The sensation is nearly always that the aeroplane is turning one way or the other, and is banked in one direction, when in all probability it is flying perfectly straight. Even when making a turn, it often feels that the aeroplane is turning in the opposite direction to that indicated by the instruments.

Until you get the habit of trusting the instruments implicitly - relying on them entirely and disregarding any physical sensations - the most extraordinary things happen; but once you get the hang of watching them, noticing and correcting every slight change of reading and going by what they say, instrument flying ceases to be tiring and becomes really interesting.

Another awkward thing is to get used to watching *all* the instruments, and not concentrating for too long on any one dial. At first one is apt to concentrate for too long on one reading, forgetting about the others, with the result that the instrument that is being watched behaves all right, while the others are all over the place and the aeroplane is doing all sorts of funny things. The instructor sitting in front, watching events, must at times have had some most hair-raising experiences!

On my first few trips under the hood I simply practised flying straight and level... or attempted to, and did some climbing, gliding, and turns. Len would periodically say - "Air speed"... "Height"... "You are turning" - or something similar. In the early stages, twenty minutes seemed a very long time, and was really tiring, but with practice it became less and less of a strain, and eventually little more tiring than visual flying.

I used to think that instrument take-offs were a wonderful feat, and was full of admiration for those who could do them. But again, the instruments tell you what to do, and when you know how, they are very little harder than taking off while seeing the runway.

Landing on instruments is more difficult, and cannot be done without special equipment unless someone is giving verbal instructions as to your position, and height from the ground, all the time. But with someone giving these instructions, it is quite possible to land without seeing the ground. I know the first time I made such a landing I was thrilled, and very pleased with myself. Len muttered something about - "Nothing to it... ", as he climbed out of his cockpit.

The idea, of course, behind all the practice we had in instrument flying, was that a great deal of night flying and all cloud flying is done while relying entirely on instruments.

Not all the instruments, by any means, are spontaneous in their changes of reading. The magnetic compass, for instance, is useless for registering your direction while turning, and has to be ignored while the turn is being made and until after the aeroplane is flying straight and level again. Both the climb and descent indicator, and air speed indicator, have a time lag in their changes of reading which have to be allowed for. At first these idiosyncrasies make instrument flying even more of a trial to the novice, but, like everything else, they become simpler with experience.

Spinning under the hood is another curious sensation, and it is not always easy to tell by feel which way you are spinning.

The correct method of coming out of a spin is first of all to counteract the spin and put the aeroplane into a straight dive... then to bring it back to its normal flying attitude. To do this you apply full opposite rudder to the direction of the spin, and immediately push the stick forward. As soon as the aeroplane ceases to spin, you centralize the rudder, and then bring her out of the dive by easing back on the stick.

All this was perfectly simple when you could see the ground, but when all you could see were a few needles swinging from side to side, or swaying up and down, it was a very different story.

There is no doubt we had come to the right country for ideal flying conditions: practically every day it was wonderfully clear, with almost unbelievable visibility. From a few thousand feet above the ground, the Rockies could be seen from anything up to three hundred miles away, which is comparable to being able to see the Lake District from over London.

I used to love that strip of changing, dazzling white, stretching nearly ninety degrees round the circumference of the horizon. It fascinated and thrilled me. Unfortunately it was forbidden territory to fly over.

Even the flat prairie horizon could be clearly defined a good eighty to a hundred miles away... not as a vague, indistinct blur in the distance, but as a clear, sharp line dividing the ground from the sky.

Our local town, Calgary, twenty-five miles away, could nearly always be seen distinctly, almost like a toy town left on a nursery floor. I have seen towns as far away as seventy miles. Obviously no details could be recognized at that distance, but nevertheless there was enough there to indicate that I was looking at a town.

This flawless visibility made navigation and map-reading ridiculously easy: too easy, in fact, from a training point of view.

There were two snags, though, that marred those almost perfect flying conditions during the summer months. The air used to get terribly bumpy, due to the fact that the ground got unevenly heated and gave off those turbulent conditions; and we used to get very strong winds... often gales. They used to start with practically no warning, and reach as much as sixty miles an hour in a very short time. It was quite common to take off in a certain direction, and in an hour's time land in exactly the opposite direction; and then possibly take off again in half an hour in still another direction.

On one occasion I was authorized up for an hour's trip. When I took off there was nothing more than a light breeze, but by the time I was due down, one of these vicious gales had sprung up. I had to use nearly full throttle to come in, otherwise I was making practically no headway.

As soon as I touched down I came to a standstill, and was then blown backwards. The brakes were not strong enough to hold, and there was nothing I could do except sit and laugh: if I had used some engine to give me forward motion I should simply have taken off again... so all

I could do was await events. I was next blown on to a wing-tip, and stayed there until help arrived.

Shortly after my aircraft had been put away, a dust storm started.

These storms also come along with very little warning: they are first seen like a dark, heavy, swirling cloud moving along the ground. As soon as anyone sees this coming, he shouts: '*Dust!*'... and everyone rushes around shutting doors and windows.

When this one was seen, our job was to get all the aircraft into the hangars as quickly as possible, and to help those who were trying to land. There were some extraordinary sights: aeroplanes descending like lifts; some hopping up and down like kangaroos; some hovering like awkward hawks a few feet off the ground. I saw one of these literally hauled down, and held down by two men on each wing-tip.

By the time the dust was on us, nothing could be seen ten yards away. It got into your eyes, mouth, nose, ears; down your neck; inside your pockets and clothes, and under the soles of your feet; it made you filthy: it tickled and scratched you. The wind tried to tear you off your feet: it made you bad-tempered... longing for a good old English London fog - which at any rate - is silent, and does not hit you, scream, and howl at you.

Those dust storms were worst in the spring, when the ploughed fields were still bare. I used to think it would be a little hard on a farmer if he had sown his fields just before the storm started, and a farmer ten miles away got the benefit of his crop. Maybe he would have got someone else's, so perhaps the result would even itself out in the long run!

The only time - barring the nights - when the air was free from bumps, was the early morning and late evening. I used to enjoy those early and late flights more than any others... particularly the early ones: the air was so clean and clear and invisible. It really was a joy, taking off just as the sun showed itself large and red and round... slowly, steadily, heaving itself across the prairie to join you in the sky.

I always used to climb facing the Rockies, with the sun behind me. The sun and the mountains seemed to play a game together, to see which could rival the other in brilliance and colour. As the sun appeared

red on one side, the Rockies would change from grey to pink: then, as the sun changed from red to light, the mountains would become blue, then white.

Even the aeroplanes seemed to delight in those grand mornings, and do all they could to help you. They would be so smooth and true in their flight, answering your every touch. There would be no sudden jolts or jumps, no sudden dropping of a wing or leaping up or falling fifty feet. If you could not fly well during those perfect mornings, you certainly never would.

You seemed to be more alone than ever, climbing into space, a space as clear and wide as eternity. The air was yours, yours to go where you would or do as you wished.

Often I used to meet birds, sometimes as high as six thousand feet above the ground. They were usually buzzards, or duck, or sometimes pigeons.

Why they were so high, I have no idea. They may have been on some long flight, and knew the wind would be more favourable at that altitude, or maybe they were exulting, as I was, in the glory of the morning, in being alive and free. Anyway, they seemed to resent the intrusion of so much noise and confusion into their freedom. As I flew past, they would flutter and jink, and I am sure their angry cries were drowned by my engine. I always felt an intruder. After all, the sky was theirs, and I was trespassing.

What a privilege, after all, to be able to join the true masters of the sky: to excel them, even, in speed, though never in movement. Your motion was only bound by your ability, and the performance of your aeroplane.

I used to long sometimes to loop and roll, but in those early days I had to wait and be content with what I had learnt.

Sometimes I was sent up to practise map-reading, or spins, or various rates of turn, or forced landings, or precautionary landings: but always I was, sorry to land… sorry that an experience almost like a dream had ended.

The mystery of flying was slowly, methodically unravelling itself: each day, each flying hour, it was becoming less involved; I was acquiring fresh skill and learning new technique. Each time I left the ground, some small point became clearer; some difficulty became easier.

I often used to wonder and marvel at the pilots of the last war, many of them in action with less hours than I already had. Was their initial skill really greater? Did they learn quicker than we were learning?

I do not know.

Probably it was a question of necessity. We had time on our side, and the hours allowed for our training. The types we should eventually have to fly were far more involved and had several times the speed of the earlier machines. I do know this: I should have been very sorry to have had to fight in those early days and in the state my flying was in, even in the slow and easily handled aeroplane X was then flying!

Any form of dog-fighting amongst ourselves was absolutely taboo. Our C.O. in his first talk to us on the day we arrived said that if any of us wanted to see the inside of a Canadian prison they had only to do some low flying or have a dog-fight. He was not pulling our legs, either! Several pupils were a bit curious, and saw the inside of a Canadian prison, and I do not think they were impressed. They came back from their stretch of fourteen days with their heads shorn!

Both dog-fighting and low flying were at times a very real temptation. You might see a friend in the sky, and long to give chase, getting him in imaginary sights, yet the memory of those clipped heads would keep you off.

Low flying was only permitted within the low-flying area and in company of an instructor. We were always told the same thing:

"Wait until you get your wings. You will get all the low flying you want then."

Those days went by very quickly, yet they were long days; days of hard work - sometimes with no time between flights. It would mean coming down from one trip, refuelling, and going straight off again. As soon as you landed; a Canadian lad would climb on the wing of your aeroplane, sit on top of the petrol tank, and bellow: "Gas truck!" The petrol bowser would drive up, fill the tank, and off you would go once more.

Sometimes there would be a wait of two or three hours for a flight.

Then there would be a visit to the canteen to buy oranges or ice cream; and sitting out in the sun, talking. That is when I heard Andre's story.

He was a young Belgian, learning to speak English, and he had been in a German concentration camp for six months. He had very harsh treatment while he was there, and all the food he got was bread and cabbage, without enough of either. During those six months he dropped from twelve stone to seven stone in weight, but he finished up by saying he would do it all again, if it meant getting to England in the end.

I am sorry to say that Andre was later washed off the pilots' course, and started training as an air gunner. I should like to have him in my crew. I met him some time later. He had completed his gunnery training, and come out top of his course with over ninety per cent. He still felt sore and rather hurt at not being able to be a pilot.

There was also a young Frenchman; he was only nineteen, and he had the M.B.E. Before he came to England he acted as a guide to British airmen escaping across the frontier.

In those early days my flying was appallingly erratic, with *on* and *off* days. There were times when I felt I was getting somewhere, and could really fly, and had confidence in everything I did. Confidence... confidence in himself, his machine, his crew, in everything he does, is essential to the pilot: he must feel he is on top.

There were days, though, when I felt none of this confidence, and when nothing seemed to go right. At times when I was up there, I hardly knew what I was doing: I did not trust myself; I did not trust the aeroplane, and in consequence I flew abominably.

The bumpy conditions had a lot to do with this bad flying. I used to hate those bumps, when the aeroplane was never steady, and you could never properly relax. They were bad at all heights up to six or seven thousand feet. At the best of times, the *Tiger Moth* is light to handle, and very sensitive on the controls; but with those vicious currents pulling at the wings or lifting the tail-plane, the stick and rudder bars were never still.

The worst part was coming in to land when the airspeed was low. A wing might suddenly drop, or the aeroplane might rise or fall twenty or fifty feet in less than a second. I used to keep the airspeed at least five miles an hour faster than I needed, and give myself plenty of room in a gliding turn.

I was ultra-cautious wnen I had those bad flying spasms, which was probably a good thing, though it could be overdone, even in those early stages. When you are over-cautious, it means you are scared... and when you are scared, you will never fly well.

Chapter XI

"We are going to do some loops to-day," Len said one morning.

"I'll fly you inverted first to get you accustomed to flying upside down."

"it sounds bloody!" I remarked.

We climbed to five thousand feet, and then Len asked: "Are your straps tight?"

I said I thought they were... and then we rolled over on to our backs.

My straps were not tight, or anything like it! They felt to me as if they were stretching, and would break at any moment. My head was pressed firmly against the sliding hood; I was off the seat, and felt as though I was standing on *my* head in space.

Len seemed to sense how I was situated, and turned round with a malicious grin.

"Not too bad, is it?" he remarked.

I did not answer.

We flew like this for a few minutes, and then rolled back again on to an even keel.

"Now for a loop," Len said. "Have a good look around first, then put the nose down. Get the speed to a hundred and twenty. Lift the nose and give her full throttle. Keep a smooth movement on the stick, and when you see the horizon behind you, close the throttle, ease her out of the dive, and open the throttle again."

As we came out of the loop we hit our own slip-stream, which showed he had kept perfectly straight.

"Now we will do one together," Len said.

When a loop is done well there is practically no feeling of movement, and nothing at all unpleasant like hanging in the straps or being pressed through the floor. There is nothing difficult in doing a loop, either: it is a straightforward and simple manoeuvre, and after doing a few I found I was able to do quite reasonable ones.

Len did not attempt to show me anything more advanced that day, such as a slow roll or a roll off the top, but was content that I should learn and practise one thing at a time.

I did not find slow rolls at all easy to learn. I could lumber around in some sort of fashion, but it took a long time before I could do anything like a reasonable one. But like most other things, they became easy with practice, and I wondered whatever I had found difficult in them. It is all a question of timing, and not allowing the nose to drop below the horizon.

Once you become reasonably confident and competent at aerobatics they are great fun, and can give a lot of satisfaction. A neat roll or loop, while being of very little practical value to the pilot, does require a certain amount of precision and timing, and teaches one a certain accuracy in flying... but most important of all, from the beginner's point of view, it gives you confidence in yourself and your machine.

To do any aerobatics really well and neatly requires a lot of practice as well as a certain degree of skill.

I heard of an instructor who was up for a C.F.S. test. He was told to do a roll. After the aeroplane was inverted it started to do everything but complete the roll. "Come on, man! you can do better than that," the testing officer shouted down the speaking tube. He got no reply, so turned round to find the rear cockpit empty and the instructor floating to earth beneath his parachute! He had forgotten to do up his straps!

While at E.F.T.S. we had to do one solo cross-country flight of about a hundred and fifty miles. It was just a question of flying to a neighbouring aerodrome seventy-five miles away, and back again.

Any form of map-reading, or so-called pilot navigation, in Western Canada, is simplicity itself. Apart from the fact that visibility is so good, the country is divided into section lines, all parallel and running north and south, and east and west. They are actually dirt roads, and in some parts little more than tracks.

These section lines vary from two to eight miles apart, according to the locality. They give the ground a singularly monotonous appearance, but are undoubtedly a great help in navigation. Even without a compass, you always have a pretty good idea of your course. The railway tracks are also a useful aid, as each 'town' has its grain elevator, which shows up like a beacon from miles away. I believe that any place, no matter how small, is called a 'town' if it boasts a grain elevator. In many cases their tall, rectangular-shaped edifices far exceed in size any other buildings, and in places appear to be the only building.

This particular trip we had to do was about as simple a crosscountry flight as could be done anywhere, as the route was roughly parallel to the railway and about eight miles from it. All the same, we looked upon it as quite an adventure, and went into elaborate preparations beforehand.

We were supposed to keep a log, and work out winds and any alterations of course necessary during the flight. This meant having a computer strapped to one knee, and a log form strapped to the other... not to mention the map. A map in the air can be a most cumbersome and annoying thing, if it is not properly folded or if it happens to come unfolded. Mine came unfolded, and was soon as much a menace to me as an aid in reaching my destination.

Each time I picked it up I found I had an unfamiliar section facing me. I had to try and refold it with the part I wanted uppermost... an annoying procedure on the ground, but in a confined space in the air...?

During this attempt, the aeroplane would wander at least thirty degrees off course, and either climb or dive five hundred feet, neither manoeuvre of much help. By the time I got the map refolded and the aeroplane approximately back on course, it would be time for another entry in the log book or possibly a calculation of course or ground speed on the computer, both procedures a further excuse for the aeroplane to meander off on its own again. Practically the whole of the trip consisted of the cycle of straightening out the aeroplane, sorting out the map, back on to course again, making an entry in the log, back on to course... and so on.

However, it was great fun, and another small step further forward.

Most people, whenever there was a question of leave or a 'forty-eight,' rushed to the Rockies. I had my chance when the whole station was given a 'forty-eight' after we had defeated the world's record for a month's flying hours for any E.F.T.S.

I went to Banff with Gibbie, one of the instructors, and Ted, my Flight Commander.

The nearest things I had seen to mountains up to then were the Scottish mountains - Ben Nevis, Ben Lomond, and the Cobbler. I had seen the Rockies from seventy miles away for the past month - and occasionally from about ten miles away when Len felt in the mood to take me in that direction - but I had no conception of what they would be like when amongst them.

I was in no way disappointed.

For the first twenty-five miles of the journey by bus they seemed as remote and unreal as ever, then gradually they became more real as they took shape. Instead of seeming to be one continuous ridge breaking the horizon, they gradually split up into definite and wonderful formations, and as we drove nearer, these formations took even more beautiful and miraculous shapes - valleys and fissures, precipices and peaks.

Trees began to appear as a dark covering round their base. Most of the mountains had this vast covering of firs, up to about seven thousand feet. Parts of the tops were hidden by clouds, which drifted nonchalantly past to reveal for a few moments the full glory of the mountains; then another cloud would slowly and ruthlessly glide across and settle comfortably round the mountain, hiding its beauty as though jealous of more being seen by inquisitive intruders. All the tops were snow-covered.

I inwardly cursed those clouds which hid our pleasure in their relentless grasp. I felt I could never see enough or tire of looking at the majesty of those mountains.

The bus stopped at a small mining town shortly after we wound our way through the first range, and everyone got out, owing to some obscure rule that the limit of a bus ride should not exceed fifty miles. However, the difficulty was overcome merely by getting out and buying another ticket!

We arrived at Banff in the late evening. The clouds had disappeared, and I had my first uninterrupted close-up view of the mountains. Wonderful!....

Banff is a typical prairie town - hideous - consisting of one wide main street running east and west, with lesser streets crossing it at right angles. It is as ugly as the mountains are beautiful, with square, flat buildings staring at each other across the main street. Most of the buildings were of the typical wooden type, with practically no attempt at beauty.

It seems a crying shame that there should not be some relationship between the mountains and the architecture. As it is there is none: it is not until one leaves the main street and wanders in amongst the trees, that one finds anything even remotely suggestive of an attempt at man-made beauty. A few enterprising individuals have built log cabins more fitted to their surroundings.

I found myself looking at the mountains and attempting to avoid seeing Banff, rather as one avoids an annoying hat in front of one in the cinema.

Gibbie proposed we climb Roundel the following day. I said nothing would suit me better, but Ted said he knew Gibbie's climbing expeditions, and would take it easily. Gibbie said there would be no climbing about it, really - only walking; but still Ted refused to go.

I, in my ignorance, was still all out for it, but felt some misgivings the following day when Gibbie appeared in full mountaineering regalia - nailed boots, peculiar hat attached to his coat by a boot lace, ice axe, and rope. I had only my uniform and ordinary walking shoes, and felt hopelessly out of place seeing Gibbie so perfectly suited to the surroundings.

I asked him what the rope was for?

"Oh, that's nothing. I always carry it."

"You don't propose to use it, I hope?"

"Good lord, no. We can walk up quite easily. You may slip a bit in those shoes, though. Pity you haven't got any boots, I'm afraid you'll get a bit wet."

Ted accompanied us for the first three miles or so, and then left us as we snaked our way along the trail through the trees.

The trails leading to the various mountains are conveniently marked by different coloured strips painted on the trunks of the trees. If I remember rightly, ours was the Orange Trail, which we were able to follow comparatively easily.

After about an hour's walking we came to the snow, and I realized pretty soon that it was 'a pity' I had not any boots. When I was not slipping backwards, I was half way up to my knees - very often beyond - in soft snow, and I was soon more than 'a bit' wet.

After another hour's walking we stopped and ate our sandwiches, as Gibbie said we were near the limit of the tree line and it would be a bit bleak further on. We did not stop longer than was necessary, as it was getting bitterly cold.

After we left the trees behind, the snow hardened considerably, which meant that I did not sink in quite so often, but slid back far more often. Occasionally I found a soft spot and sank in up to my waist.

All the time Gibbie plodded steadily ahead, ignoring my slidings and flounderings, but occasionally he would stop and wait in silence for me to catch him up. Then I would make self-excuses, usually blaming my shoes.

After another hour Gibbie said we were on the wrong ridge, and would have to retrace our steps. This was easy, as for the majority of the time it was simply a question of sitting down! After a further hour, we were on the next ridge at about the same height as we had left the old one, and continued our plodding upwards.

It was piercingly cold, with a strong wind blowing the snow around us like fine white sand. Any hope of the magnificent view I had been promised had completely gone, as at times I could barely see Gibbie thirty yards ahead of me. It started to snow, and the fine driving snow made visibility even worse. I refrained from asking the tempting question - 'how much further?' - but continued on what I had begun to consider an entirely pointless and an extremely uncomfortable journey.

We had to cross a ridge about six feet wide, with a drop of about three hundred feet on either side. I was evidently not in dead centre, for Gibbie shouted back to me:

"That's a snow cornice you're walking on!"

"What's that?" I bellowed back.

"An overhanging ridge of snow," was Gibbie's answer.

After about another hour, Gibbie stopped and waited for me. "Do you really want to go on to the top?" he asked.

"No... do you?"

"No. Let's go back."

The following day it snowed hard, and I had the luxury of breakfast in bed.

When I arrived at the hotel the previous evening the reception clerk informed me with a genial smile that he had reserved me a room with a double bed. I said I had only asked for a single bed, but he merely smiled back.

The following morning two breakfasts were brought up to me. I said I had only ordered one... and again only a smile.

I ate both breakfasts!

Chapter XII

One of the greatest thrills, I think, was night flying. Up to then, I had always looked on landing an aeroplane at night as some sort of minor miracle, though I had been landed a hundred or more times at night by other people, and had always been brought down safely and reasonably well. It was a job that did not concern me as to how it was done: I had always had sufficient faith in my pilots to leave the mystery in their hands.

But now it was different. I was being initiated into this rather weird and wonderful rite.

Len took me up as usual, with his familiar remark:

"There's nothing to it, really."

There certainly seemed to be nothing to it when he made the first landing, with me sitting behind him, watching him and having very little idea what it was all about or how far from the ground we really were.

"Watch the glide path indicator," Len said. "You can't go wrong if you keep on the green light."

"Which is it?" I asked.

I could see hundreds of lights... the flare path, the taxi-ing lights, the obstruction lights, the boundary lights, lights on parked aeroplanes - not to mention the innumerable lights in buildings scattered about the aerodrome - but which one happened to be the glide path indicator I had not the faintest idea. I was still mystified after we had landed, and told Len so.

"Look to the left of Number One flare," he replied. "I will take off again, you can fly her round the circuit, and we'll try a landing together."

I don't know how much I contributed to that landing. Probably not much.

"We'll do one more together, then you do one," Len said.

Brave men, those instructors. Not an enviable job, sitting back wondering what the pupil will do next; probably wondering what he is thinking, if he is thinking!

I was sweating, though the night was not particularly hot. Everything seemed so strange: the ground, a vague, dark something… how far below? and the river a little lighter than the rest.

There were hundreds of lights, most of them appearing to be set out in the most orderly fashion. Calgary glowed in the distance, and looked even nearer than it did in the daytime.

The whole district seemed to be awake, and I wondered when people went to bed. I could see car lights along the main highway eight miles away, houses with lights burning, and somewhere in the distance a field of stubble all alight, but brightest of all were the aerodrome lights below, and the six flares along which I had to land.

I was aware of Len sitting still and silent in front of me. He might have been asleep, he was so still, but I knew he must be very wide awake, and I felt relieved by his presence. However strange and strained I might be feeling, he would be completely at home.

We flew for two hours that night.

"Another hour, and you can go solo," Len said.

I hoped he was right.

When the time came a few nights later, I experienced all the excitements, doubts, uncertainties and thrills of my first day solo. It was a particularly dark night, or so it seemed to me, as I sat in the cockpit at the taxi-ing post waiting for my turn to take off. I went through the cockpit drill time and again as I watched, half impatiently and half rather dreading, the green light which would be my signal to leave the ground.

I wondered if any of those in front of me were starting their first solo, and if so, were they feeling as excited as I was? It was too dark to see anything but their green and red navigation lights and white identification light.

I watched these lights move down the runway and then gradually rise above the flare path. As they rose above the flat horizon I could just see the vague shapes of the aeroplanes silhouetted against the sky. It looked rather weird, watching these lights rise into the night.

My instruments glowed faintly blue in front of me. I had to lean forward to set the gyro indicator, as the luminosity was so dim that I could hardly read the figures. I preferred not to have any other cockpit lighting, as I could see better outside the aeroplane without any bright lights inside.

At last the aeroplane in front of me moved forward, and a green light was flashed in my direction. I flashed my identity letter - G for *George* - and turned left on to the runway.

Any nervousness I might have felt completely vanished as I pushed forward the throttle and gathered speed. Instead, I felt exhilaration, and pride, to be doing it: I was glad Len was not there, glad and proud to be alone.

I sang on that trip... sang all the way round. It was wonderful; so lonely, and so free. The engine seemed to be running more smoothly, and quieter, than by day. I felt I wanted to stay up for hours... not going anywhere in particular, but just flying around.

I was completely happy. Any worries I had had were forgotten: nothing mattered except the present. What was happening below ceased as far as I was concerned to exist: all that mattered was that I was up there: I was flying without realizing I was flying.

I think I felt more confidence then than I had ever felt before: I felt I could do anything; that I had some power that others had not. It was not conceit, but just a terrific feeling of well-being, that everything was very much all right, and that I was a very lucky fellow.

As I looked at the hundreds of lights below, I felt sorry for those who would never know this wonderful thrill. I felt I should like to tell someone about it; tell them what I felt, and how happy I was.

One feels far more alone and even more remote from the ground, at night. Speed and movement mean nothing; one might just as well be hovering, or be in a noisy balloon, for all the sensation one gets, in normal flight, while night flying. I have never done any gliding, but I should imagine for sheer beauty of flying - for the joy of just being up there, of being free of the ground - it must be unsurpassed, and only equalled by flying at night.

It might be imagined that the *Link Trainer* would reproduce at least some of the fascinations of flying, but to me it had no such effect. I could get no semblance of actual flying with any *Link*: I looked upon it merely as a necessary and rather monotonous part of our training.

The *Link Trainers* we used at E.F.T.S. were very sensitive and light to the touch. You sat cooped up in that box-like contrivance rigged up inside to represent as near as possible the cockpit of an aeroplane. That, however, is where the resemblance ended.

That hour to me always dragged by. I used to sit there, with the ear-phones on, listening to my instructor and watching the instruments; sitting desperately still, as the slightest shifting of position always seemed to have disastrous effects on the performance of the *Link*. Sometimes my mind would wander, and there would be a horrid, vicious, hissing sound, which was always the prelude to the *Link* doing something it should not do. Oh yes, it always warned you, as much as to say: "It is my turn now. You think of someone else, and I will show you!"

Before leaving E.F.T.S. we had to pass a final flying test. I was taken up by Ted. He was a New Zealander, large, very quiet, very gentle, very conscientious.

"Forget I'm here, old boy, and carry on as if you're alone," he said, just before we took off.

I had to do the usual things: an instrument take-off, about twenty minutes flying under the hood, some steep turns, a loop, a spin, some side slipping, a 'precautionary,' a bit of low flying, and a forced landing.

For the forced landing, Ted cut the engine at about three thousand feet, and told me to pick a suitable field and bring her in. I pointed out to him the field I had chosen, and started to glide into position for the approach. It was obvious as I was attempting to come in, that I should never make it, and would hopelessly overshoot, even allowing for side-slipping.

A soon as I saw what would happen, I said to Ted: "That's a much better field over there. I'm going in to that one."

Ted was not deceived, and I did not really think he would be. He said to me afterwards:

"I'm glad you had the sense to realize you had duffed your forced landing. You did right to go in to the next field, rather than give it up as a bad job and start all over again: if your engine had really failed, you would have had to do that, anyway."

Part Three

Part Three

Chapter XIII

While awaiting posting to E.F.T.S. I had a few days' leave, and again went to the Rockies. I told Gibbie of my intention, and he said: "I'll come too, and drive you over."

We decided to give Banff a miss, and go further west to Temple Chalet, where apparently Gibbie was well known. He assured me of a really good time:

He wired for accommodation, and received as reply: *'Unable accommodate you Temple stop Half Way Cabin available stop Bring own cook'*

"Can you cook?" Gibbie asked.

I said I was a jolly good cook.

"Then we'll go!"

We set off that very afternoon: Gibbie complete with ice axe, rope, and peculiar hat; myself with a borrowed pair of nailed boots, and wondering what I had let myself in for this time. Gibbie's other friends flatly refused to accompany us.

The road beyond Banff through the Rockies struck me as being far too well organized, and in complete contrast to the wildness of the mountains. There were notices inviting you to stop and picnic, and showing you where you could camp: there was a notice with a hand pointing to '*Typical Mountain Goat Territory*.' I would far rather spot a mountain goat on my own, than see one by following the direction of a pointing finger. However, even the descriptive notice failed to reveal any form of goat, mountain or otherwise.

This 'typical mountain goat territory' was on a barren, jagged, steep mountain face, completely devoid of vegetation, and I wondered what attraction it could possibly have for even the mountain goat.

We parked the car by the side of the road, where we should have to leave it for our two days' stay higher up, and started the seven-mile walk to Half Way Cabin, at about nine-thirty. We intended calling in at Temple, which was on our way and about four miles from where we had left the car, to collect our food.

We passed several elk and moose on our way up, and surprised a porcupine, which rushed up a tree in an incredibly nimble manner, considering its awkward appearance, with its quills rustling like dry wood.

Most of the way up we followed the pad marks of a bear. I was hoping very much we should overtake it, as I had never seen one, and we did very shortly before reaching Temple. As we rounded a bend in the trail through the trees, we saw him waddling from side to side, with his hind legs all the time apparently trying to overtake his front legs. He had a peculiarly hunched, yet very light gait.

It was nearly dark, and the bear quickly disappeared among the trees when he saw us. I believe I am right in saying that their eyesight is not particularly good, but they have a very keen sense of smell. Certainly he did not turn round until Gibbie shouted at him.

The black bear, unlike the grisly, is a harmless beast unless molested. Apparently the only way to escape a grisly is to climb a tree, but this form of evasion is no good against the black bear, who is an excellent climber himself. The black bears at Banff are well known for their tameness in the summer months, when they roam about the town, much to the delight of the tourists but to the annoyance of the inhabitants, in search of anything sweet they can find.

Gibbie rightly guessed that the one we saw was probably making its way to the garbage cans at Temple. During the summer months the bears frequently live around any habitation, and love licking out any treacle tins, jam pots, or anything else sweet they can find. They do not always confine themselves to garbage cans, either, but will wander about houses if they can find an open door or window looking for any succulent titbits. Gibbie told me that on one occasion when he was camping, he was awakened in the night by a noise inside his car. On investigation, he found a black bear seated in the driver's seat, making short work of his rations! He did not mind that so much as the fact that the bear had eaten half his prismatic compass, hoping presumably to find treacle inside!

We arrived at Temple Chalet and found the place apparently deserted. However, after some shouting and knocking on our part, the proprietor appeared. He was not in the least surprised to see us, but was extremely surprised to hear we had arrived without food or skis. The telegram as he had sent it should have read: 'Bring own *food*\ Progress beyond the Chalet, he informed us, was impossible without skis, as the snow was five feet deep and very soft.

Good man that he was, he provided us with both food and skis for our trip to Half Way Cabin, another thousand feet higher up and about three miles away. He also gave us accommodation for the night, as it was then nearly twelve o'clock.

Our host was alone in the Chalet, which was built of logs after the Swiss style, and very different from any house or cabin I had seen in Banff. He was preparing for the summer season, which would be opening in a fortnight, and it was really extremely generous of him to part with so much of his precious rations, as we knew it would mean a long trek on his part to replenish the supply.

I used to look upon Gibbie as somewhat of an expert on the mountains and the ways of the mountains, but he was a novice, a mere babe, compared to our host, who knew and loved every inch of every mountain within range of his domain. I listened, fascinated, but feeling rather like a child and very ignorant, to him and Gibbie - chiefly to him - until the early hours of the morning, as they talked of the mountains and spoke of them almost as though they were human.

Mr. White, our host, was a small, stocky man of vast physical strength, with a sad face and the gentle, kindly nature peculiar to so many men who live as close to nature and spend so much of their time alone, as he does. I felt very small and unimportant beside this man, with his infinite knowledge of the mountains, snow, animals, birds, and indeed, it appeared, of life in general.

I went to bed that night - or rather, early that morning - feeling as though I had missed a lot... as though an essential part of my life had been neglected and wasted. One can learn by reading, by talking, by being taught: but there is so much that no books, no forms of speech, can teach; that only one's eyes, ears and senses can find out.

When I heard we should have to proceed on skis, I felt even more a worm than I already felt, never having used them or seen a pair outside a shop window, in my life. Gibbie said: "There's nothing to it; it's quite simple. All you do is walk. We shall be going uphill anyway."

Nothing to it, and *quite simple*, seem to be stock phrases with flying instructors; they use them on the slightest provocation.

Our host did not laugh, or take the opportunity of flaunting his superiority, as lesser men might have done, but gave me every possible assistance in the way of tips and encouragement. Needless to say, he was very much an expert himself.

Actually it was nothing like as difficult as I had expected, as we set off that same morning with packs on our backs. True we were only going uphill, and as Gibbie put it, merely walking - or rather shuffling.

It was not long before I appreciated the necessity of our skis, as on many occasions I had to take mine off to untangle myself from the peculiar positions my frequent falls left me in. Whenever I put my weight on the snow, without skis on, I sank in up to my waist - and sometimes beyond - and it was only by contortions, and lying flat on my back or my side, that I was able to keep on the surface of the snow. Although I did not find it as difficult as I had imagined, I found it extremely hard work, particularly when on several occasions I fell over forwards, with my pack on the back of my head, burying my face in the snow. Gibbie seemed to take a good view of things when this happened, and said it was a sign of a good skier to fall over forwards, and that I was doing fine, and so on. I did not know much about that, but I did know it was jolly uncomfortable!

In due time we arrived at Half Way - a small, one-roomed log cabin, with wide wooden bunks, a large stove, bench, and table, and miscellaneous cooking utensils, china and cutlery - with myself feeling pretty tired and hungry. I at once set to work to prove my boasted excellence as a cook, while Gibbie lit the stove and swept the floor. It is wonderful what a big meal can do to revive you, when you are really hungry.

That afternoon, and until dark, I put in under Gibbie's instructions some much-needed practice with skis, in preparation for his proposed trip the following day. His suggestion was that we should cross Deception Pass and go down to Skoka, some eight miles away.

I was game for anything, anything just to be out there, to be amongst those wild and wonderful mountains. I felt it impossible that anyone could be anything but happy and enthusiastic in such magnificent surroundings.

As we smoked our final pipes before turning in that night, Gibbie told me the story of Martin's ghost. Apparently Martin, an enthusiastic but reckless skier, had set out from Half Way against the advice of those who knew more about local conditions than he did. Martin never returned: he was buried in an avalanche, where his body remained until the following summer; but Martin's ghost was said to return to Half Way at night, and roam restlessly about the cabin. The door was ill-fitting, heavy, and extremely difficult to open, but proved no obstacle to Martin, who apparently could open it with the greatest ease. He did not visit us that night, or if he did, he did not wake me.

Gibbie was up and about before it was light the next morning, and I had no choice but to follow suit.

What a morning! I do not think it ever gets properly dark, with the snow on the mountains: there always seems to be a reflected glow, with the light coming from the ground rather than from the sky. As we went outside, there was this luminous iridescence… cold and rather eerie. I thought of Martin's ghost, but he did not seem so real as he had done in the early part of the night.

I could just see the mountains, as vague, pale, lumpy shapes breaking in to the light violet sky. Gradually they took more shape as they became lighter, and more wonderful: they seemed to get bigger as they became clearer. Then the top of one slowly and very gently became pink, almost as though it was shy, and blushing to be the first among so many being noticed and chosen by the sun for his early caress.

Very slowly and carefully the rose pink spread, giving shape and attention to this mountain top, which was almost unbelievably beautiful, standing as it did alone and aloof, lit by these first slanting rays. Then the others in their turn were noticed and kissed by the soft, warm tint, until the whole horizon seemed to be smiling, gay, almost dancing, and wide awake.

Gibbie started naming the peaks, but I was not interested. To me, their names did not matter: I felt they should be beyond any such mundane notice: I felt they should be like Royalty, known and respected without the necessity for a mere name.

A grey, perky mountain jay fluttered from a neighbouring tree and came hopping towards us, showing no sign of fear or uncertainty. It hopped about at our feet, with its head on one side, peering up at us with its black, bead-like eyes.

The gophers were less certain of their safety, as each time they saw us, or each time we moved, they went scampering back to their holes among the rocks, twitching their tails as they ran. A few seconds later they would poke their heads up again, and gaze at us, evidently feeling more secure in the mouths of their holes.

The gopher is a curious, inquisitive little animal: whenever he runs down his hole, he always pops up again with just his head showing, to see what is happening outside. I have seen many caught by this foolish habit. It is simply a question of placing a running noose round the mouths of their holes, and standing well back at the end of a long piece of string. When the gopher pops up to look at you, all you have to do is pull the string and tighten the noose... and you have your gopher!

Some little distance off, two martins were chasing each other, leaving little lines on the crisp, even snow, like pencil marks on white paper. There were some bear pad marks running in a drunken manner around our cabin.

Gradually the pinkness left the mountains, and long, pale shadows stretched across the snow as the sun appeared between two peaks. When its rays glanced over the snow, it shone with a dazzling brilliancy that hurt my eyes. The snow no longer appeared flat and without form, but took the shape of minute mountain ranges, with tiny fissures, peaks and valleys forming as the sun cast a shadow from each miniature, uneven ridge.

Gibbie was getting impatient to start on our expedition, and called me in to breakfast. I was loath to go inside, even for a few minutes, as I felt that I was missing so much that I had never seen before. However, it would wait, for always, which breakfast and Gibbie would not.

Once more I clipped on my skis, and we set off, with Gibbie leading - threading our way between rocks and stunted trees, and crossing a stream by a snow bridge - and made our way towards Deception Pass. I must have benefited from my previous practice, as I fell over less often, and seemed to be making slightly faster progress. It had frozen hard during the night, and the surface was crisp and firm, and ideal for ski-ing.

We crossed a flat expanse of snow, rather like the bottom of a huge bowl, with the mountains rising all around us. I remarked on the curious flatness we were on, and Gibbie said we were crossing Clear Lake. It seemed curious to be in the middle of a frozen lake, in the last week in May.

It was soon obvious how Deception Pass derived its name. When it first came into sight, it appeared to be no more than half a mile away, although in reality it was over four miles. I found it a weary business, trudging up that long and tantalizingly deceptive slope.

At last we reached the top and stopped for a breather, and to take the skins off our skis before starting on the two-mile run down to Skoka, on the other side. I had my first view of a glacier. It was quite a small one, and looked like a great, opaque, pale green lump of ice, resting on the side of the mountain.

There may have been 'nothing to it,' as Gibbie would say, staggering uphill, but when it came to the downward run it was a very different story. Gibbie was in his element as he started with a headlong rush, turning, twisting, and choosing his path down the crisp virgin snow.

I could not turn, and the only way I could stop was by sitting down, which I did every fifty yards or so, or whenever I felt my speed and progress were getting beyond control. I found the descent almost as tiring as the climb, with my succession of falls, most of them, although not all, intentional.

Skoka was a chalet, very similar to Temple in appearance, and, like Temple, unopened for the summer season; in fact, unoccupied.

The mountains seemed as familiar to Gibbie as my own garden was to me. He gave me the name of each mountain and peak: when he had climbed that one, or when he intended to climb another. No wonder he was content to stay in Canada as long as he could. He was the only person who did not annoy me when he said he would not mind remaining in Canada until the war was over: he seemed to fit so perfectly into these wild surroundings, and anyone who loved the mountains as he did, had, I felt, almost a right to remain. He was one of the few really contented instructors I have ever met.

We reached the top of Deception Pass again on our homeward journey, with myself in a somewhat exhausted condition. I took the skins off my skis, and started on the long downward rush to the frozen lake a thousand or more feet below... slowly at first, and then, before I knew what was happening, at a terrific speed. I soon realized I was going far too fast for my customary method of stopping. I could not turn, either, and the only thing to do was to carry on and hope for the best.

For the first time, I experienced and appreciated the real thrills of skiing: I had more sensation of speed than ever before, either in the air or when riding a motor-bicycle.

The wind pulled my open-necked shirt from my chest, and half off my shoulders. The speed was silent, except for the rush of wind in my ears, and the swish of the skis on the snow. In front of me, the snow was dazzling white, and unmarked: behind, a white cloud, like the spray from a breaking wave. A sable ran across my path, and then stopped, as though surprised at anyone intruding on his domain.

At the bottom I turned round and watched Gibbie - still near the top, but coming towards me at increasing speed. 'Did I really do that?' I wondered. It seemed too good to be true. If it was not for the fact that it would take me an hour to go up what had taken me less than a minute to come down, I would have gone up straight away, just to repeat the thrill.

"You're certainly learning to ski," Gibbie said, when he reached me. "You're the first person I've ever seen tackle that slope straight down like that. I only followed you that way as I wasn't going to let you beat me!"

"It was not intentional, I assure you," I replied.

"No, I thought somehow it wasn't!"

I returned to our cabin alone, as Gibbie warned to explore a pass he had never seen before. When I got back I felt really tired, and lugged one of our mattresses outside into the warm sunshine, and lay down to sleep.

I was awakened by a brightly coloured little bird on my chest, pecking at my buttons, and shooed him away, as I was afraid he might have a go at my nose! He did not stay away for long, but returned to resume his inquisitive quest.

We had to be back at the aerodrome by midday the following day, and to make the most of our time we decided to start on our homeward journey at three o'clock the next morning. We prepared the stove and breakfast things before going to bed, so it was only a question of a match, and waiting for the kettle to boil.

It was bitterly cold outside when we started, with the snow as hard as ice and quite as slippery. The surface was cold and unrelenting, and I had no control whatsoever over our progress back. Even Gibbie was in difficulties. There was no moon, and the only light seemed to come from below. I don't know how many times I fell down, but I arrived at Temple bruised and sore, and very bad-tempered.

Mr. White was already up, and had some excellent coffee awaiting us. It was impossible to remain bad-tempered in his gentle, quiet company.

We said good-bye, and started walking back to the car, with a golden eagle circling silently above us, watching our downward progress.

Chapter XIV

There were sixteen of us in our flight; sixteen anxious, hard-working individuals struggling to be pilots… anxious because failure was not only possible, but certain, if the grade was not made.

As the course progressed, the strain was noticeable among several, but, curiously enough, less evident amongst our Allies - French, Dutch, Belgians and Czechs. Considering they had to work harder than any of us, as they were working in a strange language, this was rather extraordinary. I think probably their apparent lack of worry was due to the fact that they had already gone through so much, and had so many hardships, that they would let no further obstacles stand in their way.

One of the most noticeable among the worriers was a boy just turned twenty: Charles Ainsworth, always known as - Chas pronounced *Ches*. We soon became great friends.

I can say with absolute certainty that I have never known anyone with such charming and perfect manners. This was the first thing that struck me about Chas… it was so outstanding. His good manners were in no way ostentatious, forced, or in any way thrust at one: they were just natural, and in perfect keeping with the boy.

I know that he respected me. Respect is the basis for any good friendship.

I respected Chas too; but while he respected me for what I had done, my respect for him was for what I knew him to be capable of doing, and what I hoped he would do in the future.

He knew that I was particularly weak at aircraft recognition, which was his strongest subject - in fact, he was a real expert at it. Whenever he found me doing nothing - either basking in the sun, or sitting in the crew room - he used to come up to me, saying: "Excuse me, sir... how about a spot of aircraft rec.?"

When Chas was about I was never allowed to be idle. He was always ready with his silhouettes, photos and books, and in his charming manner used to instruct me - not with any idea of showing off his superior knowledge, but with a genuine wish to help someone.

He used to worry quite unnecessarily about his flying: he was one of the keenest in our flight, and anyone as keen and enthusiastic as he was would certainly not be failed without really good cause.

At the end of our last week at De Winton, posting lists began to appear for S.F.T.S. I was recommended for 'twins,' which was what I wanted. I had the choice of the twin-engine S.F.T.S. Stations to be posted to, and I chose -, where we should be flying *Ansons*.

Not that I knew anything about the place myself, but was merely going on what I had heard.

I was asked if there was anyone I should like to go with me, and chose Chas, as he was likewise recommended for 'twins.' He was disappointed, as I knew he particularly wanted 'singles.' Most of the youngsters preferred the idea of 'singles,' rather than 'twins': 'singles' suggested fighters, and the fighter pilot is endowed with more dash and spirit of adventure than the more sedate bomber pilot. At least, that is the popular conception.

However, it was pointed out to everyone that those posted to the single-engine S.F.T.S. Stations would not necessarily be made fighter pilots, while those posted to 'twins' would not of necessity become bomber pilots. This did a lot to alleviate the feelings of those who were disappointed in their postings.

- is on the prairies, and about a hundred miles west of Winnipeg, which, from most people's point of view, was its saving grace - particularly as we had a 'forty-eight' every alternate weekend. We arrived on a Saturday evening, and started work the following Monday.

Chas and I were put in the same flight - or rather, I fixed that we should be put in the same flight - as was also Chas' friend Ivor, a tall, fair, quiet boy, three months younger than Chas, but looking three years older.

Ivor was Chas' opposite in temperament. While Chas was always laughing, rather impetuous, very emotional, and with many friends, Ivor was serious, apparently unemotional, inclined to be over-cautious but excessively loyal, and seemed quite content to have Chas, and later on myself, as his only friends. We soon became quite inseparable, and were known as 'the three musketeers.' I took Chas 'under my wing' and made it my special and self-appointed duty to look after his welfare… quite unnecessarily, as he is extremely independent and at times obstinate! Incidentally he soon discovered mannerisms that irritated me and pulled them off whenever I annoyed him!

Some time later, when we were on leave, we met a graphologist, who set his powers to work on our handwriting. He certainly gave us an incredibly accurate and thorough account of our characters, as well as a prediction of what he thought we were best fitted to do. He said that Chas would be far more suited as a fighter pilot than as a bomber pilot - which I think is correct - and that Ivor would be far more suited to bombers, which is also correct. I asked him what type of aeroplane I was best fitted to fly.

"You… ?" he said. "You should not be allowed near any sort of aeroplane at all!"

Once again I was extremely lucky in my new instructor, Mac, who, curiously enough, reminded me somewhat of Len. At first I thought he was a dour Scotsman, but this first impression quickly vanished, for although he was a Scotsman, he was far from dour. He was twenty-one, but looked much older, with his partly bald head and quiet, confident manner.

I never saw Mac hurry, or get in any way flustered. I only twice saw him really annoyed… once, when a testing officer sent one of his pupils solo against Mac's recommendation. I saw this pupil make his first landing, and I thought that Mac had every reason to be annoyed! The second time was when someone disputed an order he gave when he was acting as Flight Commander.

On our first acquaintance, Mac was at pains to point out to me what a safe aeroplane the *Anson* was; what an easy aeroplane it was to fly, and that on no account was I to abuse these qualities. He told me I could do all sorts of foolish things with comparative safety… things that could not be done and got away with in any other type of aeroplane.

"People who fly *Ansons*," he said, "think they can fly long before they really can. Always remember you are flying one of the easiest aircraft in the Service; it will fly itself most of the time.

"You will approach to land at seventy-five, which will give you a big safety margin of speed, a thing you won't get in any other aeroplane. You'll find they are almost impossible to spin, which again you won't find with many other aircraft. For this reason, they are bad kites to train on. They are too easy, and because they are easy, I shall expect a very high standard of flying."

I liked Mac right from the start, and fully realized how fortunate I was in my instructor.

I thought the *Ansons* seemed very big, after the *Tigers*, and felt rather proud that I should soon have control of one. I really felt that flying was beginning to be to some purpose, and that I was getting nearer to what I wanted.

The first day, it rained, and was one of the few wet days we had. Chas and I climbed into one of the aircraft in the hangar to learn all we could about the cockpit layout and controls. There seemed a vast number of instruments, levers, knobs, and switches, compared with the few we had to deal with in the *Tiger Moths*. They seemed even bigger, lying idle in the hangar, as aircraft somehow always do.

The S.F.T.S. course was divided into two equal periods… I.T.S. (Initial Training Squadron), and A.T.S. (Advanced Training Squadron). In the first we were taught to fly, and in the second we were taught how to use that knowledge of flying. As at E.F.T.S., we flew alternate mornings and afternoons, with ground instruction in between.

Mac was an excellent instructor, as well as a very hard taskmaster: nothing short of perfection, or as near perfection as you could possibly get, would satisfy him. He was far more ready to find fault than to give praise, which is a good thing, as there is nothing like flying to make one feel satisfied with oneself and on top of the world - and Mac knew perfectly well that over-satisfaction, and in consequence, over-confidence, can be very dangerous things: they can make the novice do ridiculous things with disastrous results.

Mac took me through from the very beginning again... taxi-ing, take-offs and landings, and all the preliminaries necessary to the first solo.

Compared with the *Tiger Moths* I had become accustomed to, there was a lot more to learn in the handling of the *Anson*: besides having two engines to think about, there were flaps and the retractable undercarriage. That retractable undercarriage caused many people a lot of trouble.

"Whatever you do, don't forget your undercart," Mac used to say. "You've got four indicators to show you if it is up or down, besides being able to see the wheels; and for heaven's sake, check on them all. You've got the horn, which is conveniently situated just behind your left ear, and will give you earache when you throttle back, if your wheels are still up. You've got the red light, which will always be on when the wheels are up; you've got the needle indicators, which will be up when the wheels are up, and down when they are down; and you've got the green balls, which will only show when your wheels are down, so you've got no excuse whatsoever to make a belly landing. Even if you have an excuse, nobody will believe you!

"Whatever I say, or any other instructor says, there are always pupils who still persist in landing with their wheels up. I had a pupil once who came merrily in to land with his undercart up: he had his R/T on, and the duty pilot was screaming at him the whole way in to lower his wheels; but the pupil still came in, and landed on his belly.

"He was marched straight off to the C.I., who said to him: '*Didn't you hear the duty pilot shouting at you down the R/T?*'

"'*Yes*,' said the pupil, '*But the horn was making such a noise, I couldn't hear what he said!*'"

We had one pupil on our course who made a belly landing. H was taken off flying for a month, and put on aircraft cleaning for that period.

Some time later, Mac said to me: "Don't your knuckles get sore?"

"No... why?" I asked.

"Well, just before you land, you always give the undercarriage lever a jolly good rap with them."

I suppose I must have had our aircraft cleaning friend in mind!

If by any chance the undercarriage would not come down for any reason, or if any of the indicators failed to register - thus showing that it might not be locked down - the rule was that we had to 'shoot up' the control tower before attempting to land, when the crash wagon would be in readiness in case of a pile up.

It was a fairly frequent occurrence that one or more of the indicators failed to function - owing either to flat accumulators or some instrument failure - and it was usually looked upon as an excuse for an official shoot-up, and low flying. I always hoped that I should get this opportunity, and was rewarded on two occasions... once at night, and once by day when I was flying with Chas, but both times false alarms.

One of our primary exercises, and one of the most important and useful, was single-engine flying. Every pupil had to be able to fly and land on one engine before going solo.

As soon as an engine cuts, the first thing we were taught to do was to keep the aeroplane straight, and then maintain height if possible: this was done by applying full opposite rudder to the side on which the engine had failed, and by the use of as much throttle as was necessary. The *Anson* flies very well on one engine, and actually maintains height for a considerable time, or sometimes even climbs.

It is tiring flying for any length of time on one engine, as the rudder bar needs a lot of pressure to hold it against the effect of the slipstream, even with full rudder trim. The hardest thing is to maintain a good airspeed, which anyway becomes very low and can be dangerously low if it is not watched. We were given fixed airspeeds at which to fly on one engine, and at which to land: Mac was very particular about this, and used to pounce on me like a dog on a rat whenever I became careless.

Often, at the end of a trip, Mac used to make me stop before turning back to the parking strip, and say: "I want to talk to you" - and I knew perfectly well that 1 was in for it! Then he would pull my flying to pieces bit by bit, going into minute details of all the mistakes I had made.

When Mac had nothing to say at the end of a trip, I knew I had done reasonably well!

In the instructors' room there was a large blackboard, on which were all the pupils' names, together with details of their flying times. In the first week six of those names were washed off, and every week saw further erasions.

These blank spaces were depressing, but at the same time were an incentive to greater effort on our part. Far better to have a doubtful pupil washed out in his early stages while he was still alive, than to risk him killing himself later, or, worse still, killing himself with his crew at an even later date. Most of the failed pilots re-mustered to other aircrew duties... navigators, air bombers, or air gunners. Much better a live air gunner, than a dead pilot.

Many of the 'wash-outs' were due not only to bad flying or to inability to fly, but either to lack of confidence or purely psychological reasons. Some of the pupils claimed that they could fly perfectly well when alone, or with their own instructors, but as soon as they flew with a testing officer or were up for any sort of test, they went all to pieces; their nerves failed them, and they felt they could do nothing right. If they cracked when under the strain of a flying test, the chances are that they would not be any better off when flying under the strain of operational conditions; and the purpose of our training, after all, was primarily for operational work.

I don't think any of the instructors liked to see their pupils failed, any more than we liked to see our course steadily diminishing: most instructors took terrific pains over their pupils, and did everything they possibly could to get them up to scratch. I heard of one instructor whose patience was tried beyond the limit of his endurance: his pupil apparently did everything he could to kill himself and his instructor, and it was obvious he would never go solo.

The instructor did all he could, but eventually had to tell the pupil that it was necessary to put him up for a 'wash-out' test. The pupil protested, saying that he knew he could land perfectly well, if only the instructor would not take over each time he was coming in, and muck up his landing for him!

This was more than the instructor could stand, so he took the pupil up once more, and calmly sat back while the pupil piled up on landing, luckily without any bodily harm, but more or less wrecking the aeroplane!

Compared with the *Tiger Moths*, the *Anson* had quite an elaborate cockpit drill to be gone through before take-off. It was made even more elaborate than it need have been, to prepare us for the more complicated types we should later have to fly. Mac was extremely particular about this cockpit check, and used to watch me like a hawk while I went through it - enumerating out loud each control or switch that I was operating. He would never, and quite rightly, allow me to hurry through, and if I left anything out, or if I did anything in its wrong sequence, he would immediately stop me and look with a pained expression, as much as to say: *You are my pupil, and you have let me down!*

On one occasion I had been through the usual check, and turned to Mac, as I always did, to ask if he was ready for take-off.

"Not with me in the kite, you don't!"

"Why not, Mac?"

"Why not, man! Look!"

I looked, and Mac had every reason this time to appear hurt. I had forgotten the most important thing of all, the elevator trim, a negligence that had been the cause of the death of more than one crew. It was a very serious mistake, and I deserved anything that Mac cared to hand out to me.

For the remainder of that trip, I felt like a small boy who has been caught stealing jam. I make no excuse for my almost criminal negligence, for such it was.

I think Mac knew that I would not let it happen again, for he did no more about it. (*If the tail trim is left wound back, on a heavy aircraft - as I had left it - the aeroplane is as tail-heavy as it can be, and the moment it leaves the ground it will soar up until it stalls, and a man's strength is often not sufficient to force the control column forward.*)

I had the same old thrill for my first solo with the *Anson* as I had experienced with the *Tiger Moth*, only this time it was not so much mingled with trepidation as with pride. I really felt I was getting somewhere. There was I, alone in an aeroplane, capable of carrying passengers, or even, if necessary, a bomb load. I could dispense with Mac's critical eye beside me, and was considered capable of being allowed to take this expensive and, what seemed to me then, large aeroplane off on my own. Life was good, and I was happy. Even then I was imagining myself with a crew: I imagined I had a navigator and a wireless operator behind me, and an air gunner to defend me.

The thrill and glory of that first solo, however, was-only in my imagination, for it was only a circuit and landing - a mere formality really - and a prelude to more groundwork, drudgery, and more serious flying, which had to become automatic and instinctive before I should even begin to be a pilot. There were hours spent in circuits and bumps, in accurate turns, instrument flying, in single-engine flying and landings, forced landings, precautionary landings, power approaches, glide approaches, flapless approaches, and flying under all manner of conditions.

About half my flying hours at I.T.S. were spent with Mac beside me, criticizing, demonstrating, encouraging... doing everything that he knew to train a pilot. The other half was spent solo, in practising what I had learnt.

Although Mac was very young, I felt I was in the hands of a man who really knew his job. If Mac told me a thing had to be done in a certain manner, I knew without question that that was the best way: I knew that it was not just a whim of Mac's, but was the most efficient method of doing that particular thing.

After we had flown for a certain number of hours, we were allowed to carry passengers. This again was another step forward, and I felt the first pride of responsibility when I reached that stage. I felt a certain satisfaction in that I had been recognized and certified as a sufficiently safe pilot to be entrusted with the lives of other people.

We had quite a lot of instrument flying to do, which comprised flying under the hood at varying attitudes and speeds, as well as flying blind on one engine. There was no means of blacking out the cockpit, as there had been in the *Tiger Moth*, so we had to fly either with hooded contraptions over our heads, or with specially designed goggles both of which effectively blacked out all the outside view and left only the instruments to be seen. Normally on these blind-flying trips, which lasted anything up to three hours, our instructors took us on some sort of cross-country flight. Not that it made any difference to the pupil where he went, but a change of scenery made some sort of break for the instructor.

Sometimes these blind-flying trips were used as ferrying trips. On one occasion we took a football team to Weyburn, about a hundred and fifty miles away. This again made me feel that my flying was being put to some small use.

I went as passenger to Chas on one of his long, blind-flying expeditions, as his instructor wanted to fly to the 49th Parallel, which I was also anxious to see - We flew along this imaginary line, made visible by a cutting through the forest, with America on one side and Canada on the other. I don't know how far this cutting extends in its visible form, but we flew along it for several miles and could still see it stretching away in the distance like a crack on the surface of the earth.

It was interesting watching Chas fly, and watching the reactions of another pupil. I was very critical, as up to then I had only my instructor's flying with which to compare the standard of my own performance. I learned a lot from Chas' mistakes, which I was looking out for all the time, as I realized I probably made very much the same myself. Several times his instructor cut an engine, and each time Chas made the necessary corrections and went through his cockpit check systematically, and, I thought, very efficiently. He never showed any sign of hesitation or fumbling, but seemed to react instantly to the emergency and know exactly what he was about. I thought then that Chas would make a very good pilot. I judged a pilot by... would I mind flying with him? I would not mind flying with Chas.

I don't think I have ever known anyone get more pleasure out of flying than he does. He always seems completely happy, unless he does badly, or imagines he is doing badly. Then nobody can look more miserable than he does, and no amount of encouragement will cheer him up until he thinks he has got that particular thing taped. If he has had an off day, he is like a dog that has been scolded by his master.

Several times I used to upbraid him for this, but he would reply saying - *Who was I to talk, as I was just as bad myself!*

Chapter XV

If I had worked hard at E.F.T.S., I had to work far harder at S.F.T.S., not so much on the flying side, which I was beginning to find fairly easy, but at the ground subjects, which I found very far from easy. Our instructors, with the exception of the Met. men, were Service personnel, and even if they were not all first-class instructors, they did everything they could to help us both during regular lecture hours and afterwards, and frequently put in a great deal of extra time in the evenings for our benefit.

I found that I had to make full use of nearly all my spare time in the evenings, working - and usually Chas and Ivor joined me in my room, where we used to wrestle through anything that was puzzling us. Chas was the expert in aircraft recognition; Ivor was the king-pin in navigation, while I fancied myself at Met. and armament, so between us we struggled along.

About a third of the evening was usually spent in serious work, while the remaining two-thirds was spent talking and building castles in the air. I had quite converted Chas to the idea of bombers, and we three had made up our minds that we would be posted together as far as possible. On the evenings when we were not working, we usually went to *The Rex*, a local cafe, where we had a prolonged meal gorging ourselves with steak, ice cream, and milk shakes. Again more castles in the air!

I look back on those months at S.F.T.S. as the happiest I spent in Canada.

The work was more interesting and more varied than it had been at E.F.T.S.; there were so many new things to be learnt and seen. Life was good, and friends were good. There was also a squash court, and the padre and I used to have almost daily battles.

One thing I missed was the sea, or anywhere where we could bathe, particularly during the hot summer months. I did not find the heat anything like as trying as I had been led to believe, as there was usually a wind blowing, and we always had the relief of cool nights, at any rate on the prairies.

I saw the most vicious thunderstorms, which were an almost nightly occurrence, that I have ever seen. Great rolling masses of cumulonimbus used to spread themselves across the sky at night, giving these most violent storms. They were usually very beautiful, particularly in the distance, when the sky would be a series of flashes chasing up and down and round the horizon and reminded me of a flak barrage during a night raid. They were too noisy, and so often accompanied by torrential rain, to be pleasant when overhead.

I was in the mess one evening, when there was a crash outside as loud as an exploding bomb: the noise seemed to come from the ground, rather than from the sky like the other claps. About a minute later the fire engine raced up to our quarters, and 1 went outside with the others to see what it was all about. The corner of the living quarters had been struck, just by my room!

I never found flying a grind. Each time I went up savoured of something new; there always seemed to be some fresh interest, something more to see or to learn. Even common or garden circuits and bumps had their charm, as conditions on no two days were alike.

Quite early on at I.T.S. we had to pass a precision landing test, which meant touching down on a given spot on the runway. This needed careful timing and accurate judgment, and was an excellent exercise in controlling a landing - particularly as on the runway we were using there was quite a lot of length to spare, which might not always be the case in future when we would be on heavier and faster types.

Quite one of the most interesting, exciting and enjoyable items of all our work at I.T.S. was formation flying. We used to fly in 'vie' formation, with three aircraft; two pupils to each aircraft for solo work, or with an instructor for dual. I flew with Chas on his first solo effort, and an amazingly fine show he put up, too. He seemed to take to this type of flying like a duck takes to water, and I know he enjoyed it best of all his work in the air.

We were supposed to keep at a distance of two wing spans apart, although in practice this was diminished to about half a wing span - the closeness of the distance depending on the fussiness, or otherwise, of the instructor. I felt absolutely safe with Chas, even in his early stages, no matter how close he formated, which is more than I can say for many of the other pupils! We used to take it in turns leading; then after our turn in front, drop back to number Two or Three.

It is much more fun formating than it is leading; although the safety of the formation is dependent on the leader, who can take his formation where he will. The leader can make the task of his formation easy or hard by the way he flies - by keeping a steady airspeed and height, and by constant rate of turns.

There was one man who was definitely not popular as a leader. He was known as *The Clot*, usually preceded by a pretty powerful adjective!

I really enjoyed formation flying, and used to love sitting with one hand on the throttles, and with my head turned watching the leader, following his every move. On bumpy days it was quite hard work keeping station on the leader while he rose up and down like a ship on the sea, or a see-saw. The whole time was spent in continually following him up and down by pressure on the control column, in catching him up by the use of more throttle, or by keeping abreast of him by throttling back… all the time with slight movements on the rudder bars to keep in equal distance.

On the first few trips, when practically everybody was a bit rough on the controls and making rather violent movements of the throttle, the horn which sounded whenever the throttles were closed was a confounded nuisance. These movements of the throttle, elevator and rudder were at first very excessive, but with practice they became less and less, until eventually they were hardly noticeable.

The whole secret of formation flying is never allowing the relationship of yourself and your leader to vary by more than a few feet. This is where Chas scored right from the beginning: he seemed to have an instinctive feeling for what to do, whereas other pupils would be bobbing up and down like jack-in-the-boxes, and swaying from side to side like leaves in the wind. I think his success was largely due to his terrific enjoyment.

Once you let this see-saw or swaying movement get the better of you, it goes on increasing and is difficult to stop. The only thing is not to let it start, by concentrating on the gap between yourself and the aeroplane on which you are formating. Once you have got accustomed to being close to another aeroplane in the air, and have control of your aircraft, it is easier to keep more accurate formation tucked well in, than at a distance of about two wing spans, as it is far simpler to judge a distance of say ten feet, than a hundred or more feet, and to keep that distance constant.

We used to take it in turns flying and acting second or safety pilot to another pupil. The job of the second pilot was to keep track of the direction of the flight, and to look out for any other aircraft in the vicinity. It was interesting watching the different styles of flying... how pupils used to sit at the controls, how they handled them, and how they reacted to different eventualities.

We had one instructor who was very interested in his pupils' psychological outlook, and how they would react in an emergency. One of his favourite tricks was suddenly to say to the pupil: "Prepare to abandon aircraft!"

On one occasion when he had said this, his pupil clipped on his parachute pack and ran aft. A moment later, the instructor heard a door bang, and looked back to find no pupil. He really got the wind up then, and started circling and looking for an open parachute, all the time thinking what excuse he could give for baling out his pupil. To make matters worse, there was no open parachute to be seen. After a while, the pupil put his instructor out of his misery by appearing out of the rear compartment, where he had been hiding!

This same instructor taught me a lot in formation flying one day, by making me fly with my feet off the rudder bar. The fault with a lot of people when formation flying, and I know it was so with me, is pressing the aeroplane away from formation with the rudder, and at the same time keeping her straight with the ailerons. This means that the controls are 'crossed,' and the aircraft will all the while fly slightly one wing low. This was about Chas' only fault, and he even used to trim his rudder like this, thus deliberately making the aeroplane fly with one wing slightly down. I was surprised how comparatively easy it was to keep quite good formation without any rudder, simply by using aileron control. I think this is about the most useful tip I have had in formation flying: the rest is all practice. Like all other flying, you can only be shown how, and have your mistakes pointed out to you, and the rest is up to the individual.

There is something intimate and almost uncanny about formation flying that you do not get in any other type of flying. It is strange at first, seeing another aeroplane so close to you. This other aeroplane always looks as though it is hovering: you lose that feeling of remoteness and isolation you get when alone; you are not so much conscious of the ground, and in consequence, to a certain extent, lose your sense of direction.

You watch your partner all the time in this game of follow-the-leader. If you are leading, you can see him, with his head turned, watching you. He always seems to be so still, almost like a statue, with one hand on the control column and the other on the throttles, instantly ready to check or turn or slip in or out.

Accidents while formation flying are comparatively rare, and even if you do touch the other aeroplane, it is not necessarily serious, as the relative speed between the two is so slight. I have seen real experts at the game playfully tap each other's wing tips, although naturally if we had attempted any such fun we should have had to look for another job!

An anxious time for many people was our Wings Test, which came at the end of the I.T.S. course. Actually the test was mis-named, as we did not receive our wings at the completion of it and not until we had finished our A.T.S. course, so it meant we were very far from being out of the wood. This so-called Wings Test reduced our numbers even further, which caused several people some rude shocks.

There was one testing officer, Hubber, known as *Hubber the Scrubber* owing to the number of people he managed to fail. Many of the failures for some reason or other seemed to go through his hands, hence his reputation, and I think most pupils rather dreaded having him.

As I went into the classroom one afternoon, I saw Chas looking as miserable as an old nigger.

"What's the matter, Chas?"

"I had the Scrubber."

"Well?"

"I think he's failed me."

"Rot! I don't believe it. I know he hasn't. I'll find out, anyway, during break."

I went round to see our Squadron Commander. True, Chas had not put up a particularly good show, but there was no question of him being failed. Nevertheless, Chas was miserable for days afterwards, so much so, that for a short time it really did affect his flying. I think it would have hurt him more than any one, to be washed out - though God knows most of the unfortunates were miserable enough, particularly when they had got so far in their training. It took some pupils quite a lot of persuasion, even if they ever were fully persuaded, that they would be doing quite as good a job as navigator, air bomber, or air gunner. I think hurt prides must have been the worst part.

I had Hubber for my test.

I knew he went a lot by the pupil's mental attitude, and I was determined to show no concern at all, which was certainly very far from what I felt, for I was keyed up almost as though I was going on an operational flight.

I taxied round, and picked Hubber up outside his office.

"Take her away," he said, as he settled himself beside me.

He seemed to be in a talkative mood, so we kept up a continual prattle, about what, I have not the faintest idea, as I taxied to the edge of the runway. I went through my cockpit check with particular care, and turned to Hubber to ask if he were ready for take-off, and what he wanted me to do?

"Take off, and I'll tell you what to do later."

He made me do a series of climbing turns until we got to four thousand feet, when I had to do a number of steep turns and maximum rate turns. Then he cut both engines.

"Do me a forced landing," he said.

We were practically over our emergency landing field, so I started some 'S' turns and losing height, jockeying into position for the glide approach. I miscalculated the wind, and allowed myself to get too near the field with far too much height, so started some violent sideslipping, using full flap. I saw Hubber turn and look at me, as much as to say - "I don't approve, but I suppose he knows what he is doing." We were over the edge of the field, with still two hundred feet to lose. I saw Hubber's hands move towards the control column, as though he felt - 'Enough of this. He won't make it!'

This rather annoyed me, so I said: "It's all right, I've got her." He sat back.

I knew that if I mucked up this landing, it would probably upset me sufficiently to make me fail the test. I felt I had got to get her in.

I continued side-slipping as hard as I could, levelling off a few feet from the ground, and eventually made one of the best landings I have ever done.

Hubber said nothing, but I knew he approved, not by the approach, which was badly judged - but by the fact that I had landed rather than let him take over, which had obviously been his momentary intention. I felt pleased, and satisfied, and quite ready for what was to come.

"Take off again, and I shall probably cut an engine on you."

He did not do so, however, but made me do a precision landing. "I want you to do a precautionary now. Fly round at three hundred feet."

I went round with the wheels down, keeping as tight a circuit as possible, which was obviously what he intended.

"Touch down right on the edge of the runway, and imagine there is a high hedge you have got to clear."

On the final approach I kept her up at about thirty feet, until a few yards from the runway, and then closed the throttles, but far too quickly, for we dropped heavily and bounced badly. Hubber looked at me as though saying - 'Do you always do that?'

"Not good, Riv," he did say.

"I know. I'm sorry about that. Will you do one and show me how it should be done?" I felt this might put him in a good humour!

When it was my turn to take off again he turned off the petrol supply of the port engine, and the engine cut at about two hundred feet. With the port engine out of action, it meant doing a right-hand circuit, as it is dangerous turning in the direction of a dead engine, at any rate at low altitude.

It was hot and bumpy, with very little lift, and it was all I could do to maintain height - let alone climb. I had to do a very wide circuit, keeping the turns as mild as possible, as the steeper the turn the more height we should lose. Even so, we lost some on every turn.

By the time we got to the down-wind leg we had lost a hundred feet, and I began to wonder if we should make it. Owing to our wide circuit we were some way off the aerodrome, and for a horrible moment I lost it, through having to concentrate so much on the instruments. By the time we had turned into the down-wind leg there was no height at all to spare, but I thought we should just about creep in, with luck. Thank God there was not much wind.

We were about twenty feet from the ground, and fifty yards or so from the runway, when a red Very light shot across our nose.

"Your *wheels !*" Hubber shouted.

I had forgotten them... completely forgotten all about them!

Hubber turned the petrol on, and luckily the engine picked up almost instantly. Both throttles were slammed open.

I don't know who was flying, but as we climbed I turned to Hubber with a grin, hoping it was not too sheepish. He did not say a word, *and I am certain he had forgotten the undercart himself.*

"How did I do?" I asked, when we got back.

"Fair, Riv... fair. But your single engine flying is a bit ropey. You want to watch that."

Chapter XVI

I don't know what we should have done without our bi-monthly 'forty-eights.' On three occasions Chas, Ivor and I went to Kenora, on the Lake of the Woods.

I shall never forget our first visit there. The joy of seeing water after the prairies, of getting out of uniform, of having forty-eight hours of freedom and pleasure, and no work, was truly wonderful.

Kenora is a little town nestling on the edge of the lake, and almost surrounded by water. Everyone there seemed to be in holiday mood, which was not very difficult in those wonderful surroundings.

We spent nearly all our time on the lake in a canoe, paddling - it didn't matter where, just paddling - in amongst the islands. There are fourteen thousand of them, some mere rocks and uninhabited, others with houses or holiday camps, and nearly all wooded. It reminded me very much of the archipelago approach to Stockholm.

One island in particular was like a huge floating garden, with perfectly kept lawns sloping down to touch the water, a profusion of brightly coloured flowers and shrubs, rock gardens built in the natural rock, and with grotesque and gaudy Indian totem poles peeping through the trees. The whole was a galaxy of colour and splendour: one moment English, with its stately lawns; then almost Venetian, with bridges across rivulets and little bays, so that one expected a gondola to drift silently along; also a touch of Chinese, with a boat house shaped like a pagoda.

We paddled leisurely along all day, or lay back and drifted, as the mood took us. -was forgotten: we just seeped in the luxury of sun and air and freedom. The silence was superb, broken only by the plop of a rising fish or by the high-pitched, vibrating notes of the crickets whenever we drifted near an island, or annoyingly, by the discordant beat of a motor boat. When we got too hot, we stopped and bathed, either from one of the islands, or swam alongside the canoe.

Sometimes a launch passed uncomfortably close, nearly swamping us with its wash. Sometimes it did swamp us, and we would have to land on an island, empty the canoe, and dry our clothes on a rock in the sun.

Some of these islands were inhabited by Indians, where they had their low, dirty-looking tents, always a dog, and swarms of children. Sometimes we would pass them, kneeling up in their canoes and paddling at a terrific speed. The women seemed as dextrous at this as the men and we saw old women paddling along in their kneeling positions as nimbly as the young ones.

Kenora never seemed to sleep. Most of the shops stayed open until midnight, and were a blaze of light and colour.

In the evenings we used to wander down to a wharf, and watch the lights across the water. It was like a vast fairyland, with lights everywhere; thousands of lights behind us in the little town, lights across the water, reflected like golden pillars, lights moving across a bridge; and above, the stars, shimmering in their millions, but almost unnoticed.

We would stay and revel in the beauty, peace and quiet of it all until we were driven to cover by the mosquitoes biting our ankles, hands and necks. Then we used to take refuge in a cafe, and consume ice creams or milk shakes. It was a common sight to see a group of farmers or hoary old fishermen licking at ice cream or sucking milk shakes through straws. Curiously enough, they seemed quite satisfied and content.

The hospitality we received was at times almost embarrassing: there was so much of it, and we had to refuse invitations repeatedly. People would come up to us in the cafes or in the train, and ask us to meals, or to stay in their log cabins.

We found the same thing in Winnipeg, where many people throw open their houses to 'the boys'.... we were all referred to as 'boys,' regardless of age. *How are you, boys?* or - *Would you boys like to come and have some supper?*

On one of our train journeys back from Winnipeg, an old lady came up to us and said: "I have so enjoyed watching you boys." I think our most entertaining occupation was to clean our buttons! She gave us her address in Vancouver, with an invitation to stay with her if ever we went so far west. This was not an isolated case, either.

Often there were a lot of broken hearts when people were posted. A party of airmen posted home from had a large gathering to see them off from Winnipeg. Many of the men were nearly as tearful as the women.

No Englishman need ever be lonely or homesick in Canada: there is always a family willing and happy to adopt him. One lady I know, a Mrs. Pope, writes regularly every week to sixty-nine Air Force men whom she has entertained in her house. These sixty-nine reply to her letters. She writes to many others as well, who are not quite such faithful correspondents. She herself has two sons on active service overseas.

Some families I am sorry to say have had their hospitality abused, but for the most part they are ready to excuse the delinquents rather than take offence.

People seemed to know the type of hospitality we would most appreciate. Most homes were thrown open to us so that we were part of the family, and were made to feel really at home. They seemed to realize we would be happy without being 'entertained.'

I hate being 'entertained.' If I want entertainment, I prefer to seek it myself, rather than have it thrust on me. I like to be alone when I want to be alone: in fact, unless I can be with my intimate friends, I would often rather be alone. Not that I necessarily prefer my own company to that of my fellow creatures, but rather that I feel under no obligation.

I am very sensitive to atmosphere, and hate the awkwardness of strained conversations or forced relationships. We are often likened unto sheep, but we lack the sheep's placidness: I am sure that if two sheep find each other's company irksome, they simply avoid each other, and don't bear with each other with a show of cheerfulness, as we usually do. How simple it would be if we could wander off from a boring tea party, by merely saying: '*To hell with this. I'm off!*...' or say to the unwanted guest: '*You bore me. Go!*' Life would be far easier and more pleasant, and we should certainly have many more true friends. Instead, we have by convention to feign enjoyment at parties we loathe, and pretend to welcome people we dislike.

Animals are far more honest than we, and usually, in consequence, more content. They have no awkward complexes: if they feel miserable, they show it, and don't have to pretend to be gay. If a dog feels unhappy, he puts his tail down, his ears droop, and every line of him says: '*I'm unhappy*,' or '*I'm lonely*.' If you pat him, and say: '*Good dog*' he will wag his tail, if you succeed in cheering him up. If not, he will go on being unhappy until Nature exerts herself and changes his mood.

People who are forced to be polite usually say the most ridiculous things, and look utterly foolish. They are acting a repeated lie: their manner, conversation, looks, are forced. This is called being civilized. I can offer no alternative, only what we call rudeness, which would be abominable!

When I visit my friends, I like to feel at home: I don't like to be 'entertained.' I like to feel that I can talk if I want to, or listen, or even just sit. I like to be able to sit and smoke my pipe. Oh, future hosts, take heed - my pipe!

I have no patience with people who have to 'kill time,' and I know of no sentence that annoys me more than - *It helps to pass away the time*... as though life was so boring that its passage needed to be hurried. We do all we can to prolong our lives, yet we are at pains to seek means to make the end seem nearer by hastening the passing of time.

I think many people would be a lot happier and healthier if they allowed a little more time for solitude and quiet, instead of a tendency to find some sort of amusement the moment an odd hour is left unoccupied. That is probably why the average countryman is far happier and more content than the town dweller: he is very often hours alone, when he has time to think - to day-dream, which is often when one is happiest - to enjoy and appreciate the beauties of everyday things continually surrounding him.

We do not need to be artists to see the beauty we are in daily contact with. Cezanne's apples are no more beautiful than were the originals: it is only that he by his perception has arranged them in a convenient form for us to see; we are able to look at and enjoy the details that he has extracted from his surroundings and placed before our eyes. Yet that same beauty is with us all day, every day, and everywhere. One of the joys of walking is that we have time to see this continual and ever-changing joy of beauty: everywhere there are unhung and unframed masterpieces always ready for our enjoyment.

Everyone I met in Canada was genuinely interested in the happenings at home, and in the doings of those who were fighting. I have been stopped by people on several occasions in the street, or asked when I have been in private houses: "Do you mind telling me how you won your medal?"

If I had been accosted by a stranger in England, and asked the same question, my first reaction would have been - *Cheek*! - but in Canada it was somehow different: it was a genuine seeking after knowledge. So many people had little or no idea of what was going on at home, or what happened in the air over Germany, and they had a real desire to know.

When a Canadian wants something, he asks for it, and if he asks a straight question he expects a straight answer. It took me some time to realize this, and I probably offended several well-meaning people by my foolish embarrassment. In England it is more than likely I should be accused of 'shooting a line,' but in Canada I should be merely granting a simple request. I had had the opportunity of doing something which had been denied to others, and had seen things that others had not seen but would have liked to have seen, and it was up to me to share the remembrance of my experiences.

I usually feel very embarrassed when people ask me how I won my D.F.C. No doubt if I had some really good story to tell, it would be different... but I merely did what thousands are doing every day and all day. After all, flying is still a fairly novel game, and a thing that millions have never done and probably will never do.

There is still something unreal, and even wonderful, about flying, that helps to give it its romantic and rather glorious reputation.

There is something startling and very dramatic about a bombing raid on Germany, a U-boat attack by Coastal Command aircraft, or the story of some air battle. This is exciting news, and news where big results are achieved in a short space of time: it is news that sells, because it is something new, but the deeds of bravery and endurance are often far less, to my way of thinking, than those perpetrated on the battlefield or on the sea.

Fighting in the air is clean fighting. If you are killed, that is that; if you are taken prisoner, that is just bad luck… but if you are wounded, you are flown straight back to your base and deposited in a comfortable hospital, with every care and attention: you are virtually at home. But if you are wounded on the battlefield, you may have to lie for hours, or even days, in the filth of mud, in the stifling suffocation of burning sand, or in the ravaging cold of snow. When you are found, you may have to be hauled or carried to some primitive dressing station, where you may lie in agony until you can be taken to hospital, or you may never be found; you may lie unnoticed in the heat of battle whilst your friends move on. You may lie for hours whilst stretcher-bearers search for wounded amongst the dead; you may be too weak to move or shout, and only wait with tortured eyes, hoping that someone will see you.

In air fighting - at the end of a fight, or raid, or whatever you have been doing - you return to your base and live in comparative comfort and ease until the next time you are needed: you are assured of a good bed, of leave, of letters from home arriving regularly. You can go out; go to dances, shows and dinners: you can have a bath whenever you want one; shave regularly, change your clothes, have regular hours for meals and sleep, have privacy… perhaps this is the greatest luxury. True, you may be fighting your nerves all the time - which is probably the hardest fight of all - but when fighting on the ground you are surrounded by the turmoil of battle always: you move with the battle, with probably only brief periods of respite.

You may have days - or even weeks - with no chance to wash, or shave, or change your clothes; with very little time to sleep, and with only scrappy meals. For hours on end there may be the thunder and rumble of guns; shells shrieking; the repeated reports of rifles, or the staccato of machine-gun fire: the whole time there may be the uncertainty of attack; the toil, and continual moving, and, worst of all, the heart-breaking and demoralizing pang of retreat. There may be the nerve-racking hazard of surrounding mine-fields, with you expecting at any moment to be blown to eternity; there may be the devastating shattering of dive-bombing. But this is war, as so many people have known it, only it gets more unpleasant with the advancement of weapons. It is merely a development, on a gigantic and bolder scale, of the wars fought centuries ago.

People do not like to read of filth, of hunger and thirst, of fatigue and discomfort: it is something so many have seen and felt; it is something still near to some. Far better to lie back, and read of some devastating bombing raid or gigantic air battle of fighters. This is something that is not shared by the many: it savours of the unreal and novel, and in consequence has the greater appeal. Apart from this, it is something near the 'man in the street': it is something he can see: he sees aeroplanes every day; he can hear them setting off on a raid, and hear them coming back. It is something affecting him personally, for he has experienced the pang of being bombed himself.

Part Four

Chapter XVII

We passed from I.T.S. to A.T.S., and were supposed to be able to fly. We could all carry out the exercises we had been taught, with varying degrees of accuracy and skill, but I don't think any of us were foolish enough to look upon ourselves as *pilots*, although we were all capable of flying an aeroplane perfectly safely. We had been taught to fly under a variety of conditions: we could cope with engine failure; we could fly 'blind'; we could fly at night; we could fly the *Anson* according to its limited capabilities, yet none of us had been proved as pilots.

We had never been up against it... only in practice, which is a very different story. We all hoped we should cope when the time came, and I think the majority of us would, yet none of us could tell: we should not know until the time actually came, if ever it did come. We were being repeatedly warned that we were not as clever as we probably imagined ourselves to be: we were told we had reached a danger stage in our training - a stage when we were apt to consider ourselves good, and in consequence do mad things.

We were told the same thing later, at our Wings Parade. There would be plenty of time, we were told, to go mad - when it would be necessary, and we should be expected to do mad things - but until then, lay off!

There is no doubt we were at a critical stage in our career. We were independent of instructors, and in a fit state to be loosed about the country-side. It was proof to us that we were competent... but how competent? At what stage had we really got?

How were we mentally fitted to fly? When things went smoothly, and as they should, we were all more or less at the same level... perfectly safe; but if things went seriously wrong, if we were really up against it, how would each individual fare? That was a question I was perpetually asking myself.

We were an average and representative crowd of fit men, aged from nineteen upwards, and I suppose from most trades or professions.

Chas had quite given up his original dream of being a fighter pilot, and wanted bombers more than anything. Ivor felt the same, and our combined dream was that we should be in the same squadron. All very delightful, and at that time I think we believed it: at any rate we kidded ourselves we did! It was good fun and something to work for, and in moments of depression it was a sure means of cheering each other up.

I was being pressed hard to become an instructor, which did not suit me at all. I was told I was temperamentally fitted; had the right type of personality, voice, manner, and so on.

I felt flattered, but not deceived. I knew what I wanted, and was determined, if possible, to get it. I was adamant... but I always felt a bit embarrassed and sensitive about putting my true feelings to the instructors, who were doing their job, and in most cases doing it jolly well. I found it difficult to refuse with tact, and not run down what they were doing, yet I wanted to make it quite plain that their job was not for me; that I wanted to go further. (This is not intended to sound priggish, or in any sort of way running down instructors and their work. Their work is as essential as any other type of work in the air; they probably work harder than most other aircrew, with nothing, but knowing they have done their job, to show for it.)

At A.T.S. we concentrated on map reading, navigation, and bombing. The object of our flying was to carry out these exercises, and the actual flying was of secondary importance, which was a further sign of our progress. We did not have a regular instructor each, but different instructors for the various flying details.

The first exercise was in map reading. My instructor made me fly about fifty miles away from the aerodrome, and then told me to pin-point our position.

There was a railway line which I could see stretching pretty well dead straight for about fifty miles, and I could see at least six grain elevators, denoting towns, and all looking almost exactly alike. The rest of the ground was mile upon mile of rectangular fields.

The grain was ripening, and most of the fields were a soft ochre colour. Grain in Canada does not get the same glorious golden shade that it does in England, but seems to dry rather than ripen. The whole vista gave me the impression of a dried, sun-baked, rather desertlike appearance, rather than one of the most fertile districts in the world.

I pointed on the map to where I thought we were.

"All you air gunners are exactly alike," my instructor said. "You all look from the ground to the map. You must look from the map to the ground: you will find all sorts of things on the ground, that won't be marked on your map, but you will never find anything on the map that you won't find on the ground.

"Make up your mind where you think you are, then study the map carefully, and you will then know what characteristics to look for on the deck. If you look at the ground first, you will only indulge in wishful thinking, and are bound to go wrong. It is so often easy enough to make the ground fit the map, but never so easy to make the map fit the ground."

We circled a town, and he went on to point out that that particular town could be one of several on the map, but that a certain town on the map could only be the town over which we were flying.

We stayed up for two hours, flying nowhere in particular, and every now and then I would have to state where we were. My instructor never had to refer to a map himself, to see whether I was right or wrong: he seemed to know the country as well as a man knows his own back garden.

He told me afterwards that he could fly anywhere within the range of the *Anson*, and always know exactly where he was. He said he longed to have to use a map again!

Map reading after a bit became very easy, too easy, in fact, owing to the astounding visibility. Whereas in England the visibility is usually limited to a few miles, over in Canada it was nearly always practically unlimited: if we could not see where we were almost immediately, it was only a question of looking further afield, and we were bound to see some landmark we recognized.

We noticed the difference on the very few dull days we had, when we really had to keep our eyes open.

We had several tests in map reading, or pilot navigation crosscountry, when not only did our flying have to be very accurate, but all our courses and pin-points had to be exact.

My first solo effort on a pilot navigation cross-country was a trip lasting about two and a half hours. Although it was about three times the distance of my previous 'cross-country' a -, I felt almost blase about it, taking it more or less as a matter of routine, but nevertheless with great enjoyment. This was another indication that flying was becoming easier, and that I was more sure of myself.

I had to fly three legs, more or less of equal distance apart, and keep a full log of the trip - showing pin-points, drift, alterations of course, ground speeds, weather conditions, petrol consumption, and general behaviour of the aeroplane. It meant quite a lot to do, particularly as I was over country I had not seen before.

I had to map-read all the way, but, as I have said, there was nothing really difficult about this in that crystal-clear atmosphere, when every detail stood out as clearly as a nigger in the snow.

We had to do several of these so-called 'pilot navigation' trips, each one a bit longer than the last. They were all flown solo, the idea being to give us confidence, as well as practice in map reading.

On one of these trips, Chas was due to take off some ten minutes after me, and I arranged to meet him over one of the turning points and then do the remainder of the trip together. I was circling round the town where we had to turn, and saw an aeroplane approaching, which I took to be Chas.

I turned to meet him, and gave my usual signal of waggling my wings, but each time I tried to formate, the other aeroplane turned away. In the end I gave it up as a bad job and wondered what on earth Chas was up to, but I continued keeping him in sight, until I did not think much of his course, so went off on my own.

On returning, I found Chas in the crew room, looking very fed up. He had not taken off, as his aeroplane had gone U.S.!

Besides those solo pilot navigation cross-country's, we had to do a number of D.R. trips with another pupil acting as navigator. Chas and I always worked together, doing alternate trips as pilot and as navigator.

Chas hated navigation, and I shall never forget his first trip in that capacity. We had been flying about half an hour, when I looked behind me to see Chas staring ahead… looking utterly dejected and miserable, as only he can look when things go wrong. I burst out laughing; I could not help it. Poor old Chas, he had completely given up, and I could see his dreams of being a pilot fading!

"Come and fly, Chas, and let's have a look."

The look of gratitude he gave me as he came up to change over repaid me for anything I could do for him and was far more eloquent than any words could be. He had complete faith in me, and I pray God that faith will always last.

Five minutes later Chas was happy again. He was flying, and I hope felt that his plot was in good hands!

I mention this, as now the boot is on the other foot, and it is I who look to Chas for guidance in navigational problems. Although he still maintains he hates the game, in my opinion he is exceptionally good, and if it was not that I know how he loves flying I would somehow get him as my navigator, but I know he would hate me if I did!

When my turn came as navigator, we ran into cloud about fifty miles from the aerodrome. Chas climbed through the clouds, and we flew for some time just skimming the tops.

When flying across the white, billowy tops of clouds, looking rather like rolls and balls of cotton-wool, it gives an impression of low flying - and a true impression of speed, which is always lacking at any reasonable altitude.

Flying above cloud without an instructor was not allowed.

"What shall we do?" Chas asked. "Do you think we ought to turn back?"

"You're captain, Chas. I'm game to go on, if you are."

"O.K., let's go on. It might only be a bank, and we can drop down the other side."

We flew for about twenty minutes, without seeing any break, and I suggested to Chas that we have a look below.

"Better take it carefully," I said. "I hope I know where we are, but there are some hills, not far off."

I gave him the height of the ground over which I thought we were, and he made a gentle descent, watching his altimeter.

We broke cloud about a hundred feet from the ground, and, as Chas put it, almost riding a horse… so climbed up again pretty quickly. Rather than turn back, we thought we would fly to the end of our second leg, and see what the weather was like there. We were both enjoying ourselves far too much to go home.

I gave him a fresh course to fly, and we continued until the clouds broke, and completed the remainder of the trip.

One of the most amusing and interesting of these D.R. cross-country's was a sealed orders trip. The navigator was given a sealed envelope, which he had to open when air-borne. In it was a series of courses, air speeds, and heights at which to fly. His job was to plot these courses, and give them to his pilot: the pilot had to map-read, and keep his own log.

Chas got into his usual navigational difficulties, and eventually we were away from the maps we were carrying.

"We're off the map, Chas!" I said.

"Do you know where we are?" he asked.

"Vaguely. We'll carry on, though."

I could see Lake Winnipeg in the distance, and anyway, in an emergency we had only to turn to the starboard until we hit the main railway line, which was the only double-track line in that part of Canada, so it was practically impossible to get really lost.

Neither of us was in the least worried, but looked upon it as great fun. We both had the reputation of making our trips last longer than anyone else, and as we both enjoyed them it was also great fun.

We ran into several bad storms, which added considerably to the interest of the trip and gave me the opportunity of some unofficial blind flying.

Without doubt the most thrilling of all our cross-country's were the low-flying trips, which were always done in the company of an instructor. The one I enjoyed most of all was the three hours' flight: I was thrilled from beginning to end.

The lower one flies, the harder it is to map-read, as one's range of vision is considerably decreased, and when really low the view one gets is no more than from an upstair window or from the higher branches of a tree.

This trip consisted of four legs, each turning-point being a small town. Before setting out, I studied our route very carefully and noticed any prominent landmarks on or near our track, as it was essential to have a preconceived idea of what to expect. Besides one's range being so limited, it is impossible to do any prolonged studying of a map whilst low flying, as one can do when higher up, for obvious reasons. A mere glance is usually all that is possible. Landmarks come and go almost before you realize they are there.

I marked our track with a heavy pencil line, and divided it into ten-mile stretches, so that I should know more or less where we were, at a glance.

This flight had to be carried out as a mock operational trip, and all towns regarded as defended areas, and all farms and isolated buildings as gun positions which had to be avoided.

I flew with my Flight Commander, Bob, who I am glad to say let me fly my own way. By that I mean - as low as I wished.

Regulations as regards 'low flying' were frequently being changed, and the heights laid down at which we were supposed to fly varied from three hundred to zero feet.

From the 'low flying' point of view, three hundred feet is of practically no value at all. In the first place, it is within range and in view of most types of guns. In the second place, it is not much more difficult flying at three hundred feet than at three thousand feet, or at any other height for that matter, whereas flying a few feet from the ground does require a great deal of judgment, skill, and concentration.

Judged from the operational point of view, the lower you fly the safer you are, as the lower you are, the more are you able to take advantage of every bit of natural cover available, and are within only limited range of vision from ground observers.

I was in a railway carriage when a formation of *Spitfires* flew past, doing some really spectacular low flying. A dear old lady next to me said: "*I suppose they must be learners.*" I think she thought that as training progressed, so did the height!

On this trip with Bob he gave me a free hand. I was on form that day, and don't ever remember enjoying flying more. The whole time we were a few feet only above the ground.

The Met. wind was considerably out, and on the first leg we drifted off our track, so much so that we had to climb to about three hundred feet to have a look around for a pin-point.

When low flying, you get the maximum feeling and thrill of speed. Imagine travelling in a motor car at well over a hundred miles an hour on an invisible road just above the woods and fields... a road undulating like a switchback with the country; a road with no restrictions, no speed limit, and no boundary; a road that would take you in any direction or to any place.

The effect of the wind is very noticeable when low down, particularly if there is a side wind, when the drift gives an aeroplane a distinct crabwise motion which is apt to be a bit disconcerting until one gets used to it. The tendency is to try and correct this drift, with the result that the aeroplane, instead of flying straight, will actually be skidding.

Birds are a bit of a menace, as they are when driving at speed along a country lane, and I am sorry to say several are usually slaughtered when low flying. Although you can see them well ahead, they are almost impossible to avoid: they never seem able to make up their minds which way to go, or which way to let you pass. They jink about all over the place in the most confused and fluttered manner, and then as you fly past they seem to shoot by, like pieces of paper blown from a railway carriage window travelling at speed.

Whenever I am low flying, I always feel keyed up and thrilled beyond words.

It is the most exhilarating feeling I know - with the possible exception of skiing - skimming just above the fields, trees, hedges, and lakes, taking everything in your stride. It gives you a feeling of superiority, power, and recklessness, and the temptation to do mad things is almost overpowering... hence the reason why pupils are not allowed to fly low without an instructor!

Details flash through one's mind like jumbled pictures on a movie screen. We chased, and rapidly overtook an elk, leaping and bounding along. A coyote ran away from us in a confused fashion. But, most vivid of all, I remember noticing some butterflies, looking so delicate and graceful, until they became mere smudges on our wind-screen.

The reactions of people we passed over were interesting. Nearly everyone stopped and stared. Most of them seemed pleased to see us, and waved. I always waved back. Some children returning from school jumped up and down in their excitement, and I dipped a wing to add to their thrill. A farmer, riding behind his tractor, did not hear us until we were alongside; then he took off his hat and waved.

Some cattle in a neighbouring field went scattering off with their tails in the air. Some ducks feeding in the rushes on the edge of a lake, rose all together, leaving the water churned in their wake.

Some people no doubt looked upon us as rowdy intruders, probably not realizing the necessity of our flight.

On the last lap Bob said: "Imagine there's a fighter on our tail."

For the next ten minutes I enjoyed flying - only 'enjoyed' is inadequate to describe my ecstasy - as I have never enjoyed and appreciated flying before. We were over some heavily wooded country. All the time I was kicking on the rudder bars, skidding and jinking, doing everything I could to evade an imaginary fighter.

At no moment was I letting the aeroplane fly straight: never did I give our imaginary foe a sitting shot. We dodged behind the clumps of trees, keeping down wherever I saw cover available.

I should have been scared with anyone else at the controls, as I am in a car whenever I think the driver is being reckless; but it is quite a different story when you are doing the things yourself! I felt then a terrific confidence; felt as though I was capable of practically anything.

I don't know what Bob's feelings were beside me, but I think at times he must have been itching to take the controls himself. I think he showed great self-restraint sitting merely as a passenger, as the thrill of low flying, particularly when one is doing it oneself, is fascinating in the extreme.

When we got out, Bob said to me: "Some really excellent flying, Riv."

I was pleased that he said this, as I knew I had done well, and his praise bucked me up no end.

Chapter XVIII

We had to do a few night flying cross-country's, both pilot navigation and D.R. trips. Again Chas and I flew together, alternately as pilot and as navigator.

There was nothing difficult in these night cross-country's, particularly the map reading ones, as every town was visible from miles away as a glow, or sparkle of lights, and our own aerodrome beacon could be seen from very nearly fifty miles away.

One trip was to Winnipeg.

Shortly after we were airborne, a glow appeared on the horizon, almost like the last remains of a sunset. As we flew in the direction of this glow it got brighter, until little tiny pin-point lights could be seen, not so much as individual lights, but rather as a suggestion of stars in the Milky Way.

Later, these lights showed like little dots of white arranged in rows, all perfectly straight, and all in perspective. These rows were crossed by further lights, until the whole looked as orderly as a carefully and accurately sown field of corn, when the rows are just appearing as straight and level lines.

When we were above the city, it shone in all its magnificence. The thousands of street lights, shop lights, lights in houses, and lights on cars, shone and twinkled, and seemed to be dancing up and down. Round about the coloured advertising signs shone in reds, and blues, and greens: they seemed to jump along the ground, playing hide and seek between the white lights. I could not see any buildings, only lights.

We flew around, enjoying ourselves.

The Northern Lights were usually a very wonderful sight. They were never the same, either on two successive nights, or for a few consecutive seconds: they stretched and wriggled and blazed across the sky, taking the most fantastic shapes.

Sometimes they would be almost blue, like a blue wave rippling across the sky, and other times they would be like a series of searchlights, crossing and re-crossing and threading their way amongst each other: sometimes the beams would be straight, then bend and intertwine. At other times they would be like a soft glow: sometimes bright... then dimming... then splitting up and dividing like vast cities in the sky; then merging into weird, uneven shapes.

I had seen them before, when flying over Northern Germany. Then we used to look upon them as a menace, giving us too much light and making us a target for the night fighters, but this time I could enjoy them for their beauty.

About a week before the end of the course, I went to see our Squadron Commander, to try and get the latest *gen* regarding our postings.

"What can I do for you?" he asked.

"Quite a lot, I hope, sir. Have you any news of our postings?"

"Not yet, but I can tell you what *you* ought to do. You are cut out to be an instructor," he replied.

"I'm afraid I don't agree, sir."

"I can't help whether you agree or not. That's what you're best suited for."

"But you know I want to go back on to Ops," I remarked.

"Look here, Rivaz... it's not what *you* want. Who are you fighting this war for?"

"My country."

"Exactly," I got in reply. "And it is our job to decide how you can best do that. We want instructors, and we want the best flyers as instructors. You have got all the necessary attributes: your flying is above the average; your voice is good; you can put things clearly, and you have the right sort of personality."

"I feel very flattered," I answered. "But I still don't agree about instructing. Surely these qualifications are just as important for the operational pilot?"

"Agreed... but if we have to train operational pilots, we must have the best men for the job."

"Surely," I pointed out, "it is rather putting the cart before the horse. You say you are training operational pilots. These operational pilots should be the best pilots. How can they be, if you keep your best men as instructors, and only send the next best home? If you made me an instructor, I should be a bad instructor: I should always be pining to get back."

"Everyone feels the same. Don't think you are the only one who comes to see me. They all do... and they all have the same plausible arguments as to why they should be sent home. Most of the instructors themselves want to get home. I want to myself, but I'm too old. I'll tell you this: I've made twenty-seven applications to be sent to a squadron, and I've given it up as a bad job."

"But instruction's your job," I retorted. "It's what you know. You've been at it for years, and you would be wasted doing anything else. You *know* the job."

"Maybe, but I'm learning all the time."

"So's everybody else. If you made me an instructor, I should have to start all over again. I should be an absolute novice, whereas I do know a little about bombing."

"I see you've got it all worked out." He laughed. "But you're not a bit convincing, you know."

"I'm being very serious, though. I would sooner go back as an air gunner than stay as an instructor."

"I don't believe for a moment you are in earnest."

"I am, sir, and I'll chuck in the course here and now if there is any question of instruction."

"In which case I hope you get shot down!"

"That would be nothing new. I'll come and see you later, if I may, sir, about the posting."

I waited a few days. They were anxious days, and I was getting worried.

The postings came through a few days before our Wings Parade. Chas, Ivor and I were posted together to a specialist course on Prince Edward Island.

I was more pleased than they were: pleased because I felt I had won my battle, and was definitely a stage further towards what I wanted. They were disappointed, as they had both set their hearts on going home straight away. However, we were all happy in that we should still be together for a little longer.

At long last the big day arrived... the day for which we had been working and waiting. Never before were buttons so bright, shoes so clean, trousers so carefully pressed, or hats so correctly worn. The day for our *Wings Parade* had arrived.

We had a rehearsal in the morning, when we were paraded, and sized, and marched on to the parade ground in the form of a hollow square.

In the afternoon, when the big moment came, we were paraded as in the morning and marched to the tune of the Station Band to our hollow square, where we awaited the arrival of the visiting Colonel who was to give us our Wings.

When our names were called, we marched up and stood before him.

I went up wearing my A/G brevet for the last time. I saw the Colonel hesitate as he reached forward to pin on the new wing.

"What shall I do with this one?" he asked.

I refrained from the obvious reply, but suggested it might go on top of the other one. As he pinned it on, he mumbled something about - "*I need not tell you how to wear it*"

That evening we had a dinner in the town, followed by a beery party on the camp, where everyone was everyone's friend, and extremely happy. The last thing I remember was turning somersaults on the grass, and climbing a hangar roof!

Chapter XIX

Before going to Prince Edward Island, we had a fortnight's leave, and I think we needed it. Speaking for myself, I was very tired, and badly in need of a rest. The course had been a great strain, and I had had to work extremely hard.

Chas, Ivor and I went together to stay with my relations in Ontario. Everyone was extremely kind, and out to give us a good time: we were out to have a good time, and intended to make the most of our leave.

One day we were driven through the vineyards and peach orchards to Niagara Falls, a sight it would have been a pity to miss while we were within easy travelling distance. I had seen them before, and took rather the pleasure of a child showing his toys to a friend, when going there with Chas and Ivor.

We did everything that trippers should do.

We stood and gazed, and no one can help but marvel at that mighty multi-coloured wall of water, falling two hundred feet to the swirling river below. There is nearly always a rainbow curving round the Falls. Flowers grow in profusion in the surrounding gardens, and the grass is always wonderfully green owing to the continual spray.

We took a trip in a little powerful steamship - *The Maid of the Mist* - which rides tossing and struggling against the rush of water at the foot of the Falls until she can go no further, and then gets swept back to take on a fresh load of passengers.

We arrayed ourselves in the long black rubber coats supplied for protection against the spray, and watched our progress below this thundering cliff of water, deafened by the roar, and wetted by the spray. When we got as close as the little ship could take us, it was like being inside a cloud, the spray was so thick. We could barely see the water ahead of us, and stood dripping and marvelling.

We had four days in New York, and flew there from Toronto.

Unfortunately an aerial view of the city was not allowed, as before we came within sight of it all the windows were curtained until after we landed.

We had an introduction to an American doctor living in New York, who met us at La Guardia airport and ushered us into the most sumptuous car I have ever seen, and then took us by a circuitous route, giving a sight-seeing commentary as we drove at speed, over bridges, down avenues and streets, and eventually through Central Park.

We stopped for a breather at our host's apartment, where he 'bought us a drink.' Americans never 'give' you a drink; they always 'buy' you one.

Having had our drink, and admired his apartment, the view, his wife, sister-in-law, and two kids, we again got into the car - accompanied by the wife, sister-in-law, and two kids - and really started in earnest to see New York.

And we did see New York!… And how! Broadway, Fifth Avenue, Times Square, The Bowery, Harlem, rushed by and became a reality, not just familiar names read or seen on the screen.

We drove to Coney Island. It was as noisy, crowded and colourful as I had imagined. We rode on the roundabouts, ate hot dogs - pronounced *dorgs* - and bought peanuts from the street vendors whose steam whistles were shrieking shrilly. The whole while, our host talked, and told us where we were; what we were seeing; what happened there; when it was built; why it was built; the height of the tallest buildings, and how many windows those buildings had. I remarked on his knowledge, and he said: *"I've lived here for forty years"*

By the time we were dropped at our hotel, we must have driven fifty miles and seen in the space of a few hours what it would have taken us days - or possibly weeks - to have seen on our own, even if we had had the energy. It was a rush; but how could we have seen the whole of New York in one afternoon if we had not rushed?

Our host was determined that we should miss nothing that he could show us. We were his guests, and he saw to it that we were the guests of New York.

That afternoon we could have had anything for the asking. We passed a vast fruit store, and I said *Gosh*! - or words to that effect - *What a sight*! He immediately stopped the car, and filled what little space was left in it with every type of fruit he could buy!

My opinion - and I know it is not shared by many - is that New York is the most beautiful city I have ever seen. It is a city of contrasts: of massive, tower-like buildings stretching like giant steps to the sky; of medium-sized apartment houses - I did not see any small houses; of lavish, expensive mansions next to poor and dingy district. The whole time I was there I felt slightly dazed by it all… almost as though I was in a dream.

I thought parts of New York were very like London. Several times I could have imagined I had turned into Regent Street, or Oxford Street, or was walking through Chelsea. It was not until I looked up that the illusion went.

I had the impression the whole time of being surrounded by bright colours, almost in a way like being in a garden. The multi-brightly-coloured taxi-cabs, roof gardens, and gaudy awnings gave this impression.

I did not seem to notice the people so much as the buildings. This was no doubt due not only to the vastness of the buildings, but probably to the fact that the people were like any other people: they would have needed to have been green or yellow or blue before they could have taken priority notice!

One of the first things that struck me was the luxury of the cars, and the brilliant way in which they were kept, and I noticed on going back to Canada how drab the cars there appeared by comparison.

On our first night we went to *Stage Door Canteen*. We had heard so much about the place, that we wanted to see it.

We wandered round for a bit, feeling rather dazed and oppressed by the crowd surrounding us. Our first impression was of a seething crowd seen through a haze of smoke.

Then we were taken in hand by a hostess, and joined a party at a table. Introductions began. I was introduced to an American corporal:

"Tom... meet Dick."

"Glad to know you, Dick."

"How are you, Tom?"

Where else, I wondered, could such delightfully informal and easy relations between ranks take place? This small incident was typical of the spirit of the Canteen; in fact, of most of the clubs we went into, and indeed of New York itself.

Everywhere we went, people went out of their way to give us a good time: theatre tickets, tickets for broadcast shows and dances, were there for us; girls were waiting for us as dancing partners. The American flair for organization was very evident, particularly, I think, amongst the women, who ran most of the clubs, and looked after us in a charming manner.

We met Lana Turner at a night club and I asked our waiter if he got a kick out of serving people like her.

"I would rather wait on you boys," he replied; and I think he meant it.

We went to the *Air Force Club*, where we met Miss Gretchen Green, that much-travelled and delightfully amusing American lady.

As soon as you come in contact with Miss Green, she takes you in hand, and you have no further say in the matter. And you are really in capable hands!

She asked us where we were staying.

"The Hotel."

"How much are you paying?"

We told her.

"That's too much," she said. "You must go to Mrs. Bell. I'll ring her up right away."

That night we stayed with Mrs. Bell.

Miss Gretchen Green is always helping people. It is her life.

She asked us what we wanted. Chas said he wanted to go home!

That, however, was beyond even her powers of organization; but she did tell us how she cured a home-sick sailor, at a loose end on fourteen days' leave. He used to be a slaughterer, so Miss Green arranged with a slaughter-house, where the sailor contentedly slaughtered sheep for fourteen days.

We talked about conditions at home, and I remarked on the shortage of paper. Within half an hour three oil-silk waistcoats arrived, stuffed with reams of a variety of paper!

Ivor remarked he did not wonder she has never married… meaning nothing but a compliment, that a woman with so full a life would be wasted on any one man.

Miss Green started, and organizes, *The Whole World Club*, where anyone in the Service is welcome. If you go there at about four p.m. you are given tea - made as in England, they truthfully claim - as well as a most homely welcome. In fact, you might be having tea in any English private house … a soothing relaxation after the somewhat hectic time anyone on leave in New York is bound to have.

Money was our main problem, and, to a certain extent, the lack of it marred the full enjoyment of our stay there.

We were told before coming to New York:

'Money… you don't want money in New York. Nobody takes any money with them to New York, and most people come away with more than they went in with'

That may be so, but I should like to know how it was done. We may have been mugs - I don't know - but we were certainly confoundedly short, and towards the end almost desperately so.

How anyone could stay in New York without spending money, I don't know. We could not, and every few hours we had to have a budget meeting.

Our problem was alleviated in a minute manner while at a broadcast show. We were given tickets, and decided to go.

We sat in the auditorium of a large hall, facing the stage. All the actors and actresses were on the stage, entertaining us in an informal manner before the show started. In a glass box by the side of the stage was the producer, with his script, watching the clock.

Just before the show started, volunteers were asked on to the stage to take part in a contest, with money prizes.

Money…!

We were on that stage like a shot out of a gun!

We were seated on chairs round the edge of the stage, and told to laugh when signalled to do so; stop when stopped; clap when ordered to; and again stop on the command.

The producer in his little box waved his arms violently, and pointed. The satellite bn the stage mimicked his actions, and the show started by the audience bursting into peals of laughter... not at anything funny they had seen or heard, but because they were told to!

More wavings of the producer's arms - repeated by his Number Two - and the laughter ceased. There were songs and jokes, and people were asked what they thought of some breakfast food, and the programme? They replied that they always ate it, and always had the radio on at that hour and never missed listening in.

We were prepared to say or do anything for a few dollars!

I was called before the microphone, and was told that if I repeated a tongue twister three times, very quickly, I should earn a dollar.

I got the dollar!

I was then told I should get another one if I repeated the same thing six times, and even quicker.

I asked if I should lose the dollar I had already earned, if I failed, and was assured the first one was perfectly safe, so in due course I pocketed the second one!

The same with Chas and Ivor. Our lunch was paid for, anyway!

Everywhere we went people were extraordinarily friendly. Several times we were stopped in the street and asked how we were getting on, or just be wished luck. One man stopped me on Broadway, and asked:

"Will you do me a favour?"

I said I would if I could.

"Then shoot Hitler for me."

We shook hands.

Now for some general impressions of Canaca... most of them first impressions, which are usually more vivid though they are apt to be more inaccurate.

It is far simpler and quicker to buy a railway ticket from London to the North of Scotland, or to the remotest part of England, than it is to purchase a bus or rail ticket in Canada for a distance of thirty miles.

I never succeeded in fathoming the system of rail tickets out there, which struck me as being complicated in the extreme. A ticket consists generally of a long strip of paper, parts of which are taken from you at various stages of the journey. Besides this long strip, you also have sundry odd pieces of pasteboard. I always used to carry all these in an envelope, and tender the whole bunch when necessary, trusting I should be left with what was required.

The shortage of public conveniences in the towns struck me as being deplorable, particularly in a country as cold as Canada in the winter.

I suppose every visitor is struck by the language. I was amused by one notice displayed outside a garage: *We fix flats*: certainly very concise, and I suppose simpler than the more pedantic - *Punctures repaired here*. Another sign frequently displayed was - *Eats*: also concise.

If you like your beef underdone, you must ask for it *rare*. If you ask for it *underdone*, you will be stared at, and probably have - *Pardon?* shot at you. I got quite used to hearing - *Pardon?* after every request I made in a shop or cafe.

If you want some sticky stuff, and ask for gum, you will be served with *chewing gum*. You must ask for *adhesive*. Sweets are always *candies*, and biscuits - *cookies*.

A tram is unheard of: it is a *street car*: and a goods train is a *freight train*.

On a railway station you don't ask for the platform number - you inquire which *track* the train is expected at. This is logical, as there are no platforms. You stand on the track, and climb on the train by steps, which are handed out by the Negro attendants at every stop.

The system of carrying heavy luggage while travelling, is, I think, far more efficient than our own. In fact, it is one of the few things that I thought superior to our methods at home. You *check* your luggage at the railway station… when it is taken off your hands, and you won't see it again until you arrive at your destination - no matter how many days the journey may take, or how many changes of trains are involved.

It is useless putting your shoes outside your bedroom door at an hotel at night to be cleaned: they would probably only be pinched, anyway! Instead, you visit one of the innumerable shoe-shine booths, where as a rule you get a magnificent shine. Negroes are the best at this game, and do a great deal of the work with their bare hands.

Hair-cutting is more expensive than I have known anywhere. It is easy to spend over two dollars by the time you have had a hair-cut, with the usual extras, together with the inevitable shoe shine.

When a Canadian wants to move house, he can do so literally, if he so wishes. The house can be jacked up on wheels and towed to another part of the town, if the owner so desires. All that remains behind is the cellar, which is in readiness for some other house. One lady told me that she had her house moved to the other end of the town, and not even put away any of her ornaments, none of which even shifted.

I asked a Canadian visiting England for the first time, what were his first impressions?

"The neatness of the country-side," he said.

I think I should say the reverse of Canada, and add - *The drabness of the colour*. Even on the sunniest days there is a singular lack of colour. I never saw any clear rivers: they were all, with the exception of some small streams, muddy and opaque. In fact, the only clear water I saw was at Clear Lake, in Manitoba.

Chapter XX

We arrived at Prince Edward Island much refreshed by our leave, and ready for further effort.

It was with somewhat of a shock that I found myself committed to Coastal Command, as I had not fully realized that this particular course was a speciality for that Command. On my inquiries as to whether it was possible to transfer to Bomber Command, I was told: "Wait until nearer the end of the course," as much as to say: 'You might change your mind by then!'

It was on this course that Chas left me standing, particularly in navigation. He went ahead like a house on fire, while I doddered along in a very slow manner.

Once again, I found working for an examination a great strain. I know that if I had been able to work at the same subjects without the feeling the whole time at the back of my mind that I had to pass an examination at the end, I should have done far more useful work. In my opinion it would have been a far better principle to have relied on the individual's honesty to work to the best of his ability and accumulate all the knowledge - really useful knowledge - he possibly could; whereas under the existing principle, any form of work which involves the passing of an examination is bound to revolve round the final issue, regardless of what might be the most valuable knowledge.

If a man worked on the same syllabus, without the worry of an examination at the end of his course, I am certain his knowledge would be every bit as great, and probably more useful. After all, when all is said and done, it all boils down to the fact that the stuff we learnt was given us to help us live longer - or to keep our crews alive longer.

As it was, my main concern was to pass the course, and to do so I had to pass the examination, with the result that the bulk of my learning was with that view in mind.

I found ship recognition one of the hardest subjects. We were supposed to distinguish every class of ship, together with the names of individual ships, of five navies.

Had this been a subject which could have been taken rather as a compulsory hobby than as a compulsory examination subject, I am certain I should have learnt more; or at any rate, what I learnt would have been of far more practical use. As it was, I had to concentrate - and I was not the only one - on the immediate issue, exams., with the result that I learnt, or tried to learn, the ships as models rather than as real ships. I found myself, for example, remembering a ship because it happened to have a broken mast, or was painted a slightly darker shade of grey, or by some other ridiculous manner... which of course was valueless from a practical point of view.

I mentioned my view to our C.I., and got a good rocket in reply! The argument against my theory is, of course, that human nature being what it is, people won't work unless there is an exam, at the end. But in this case the issue is far too important for them to do otherwise.

Towards the end of the course, our Squadron Commander sent for me.

"I'm going to try and get you transferred to Bombers," he said. "You are obviously a man of action, and the sort of person who doesn't mind flak and searchlights, and that's where you ought to be."

I wanted Bomber Command, and he knew it, but how wrong he was about the brave lion amongst the flak and searchlights. I hate loud noises, and violence!

Why do I want to go back to Bomber Command? I have often asked myself that question.

I have no need to go back. I can get a comfortable job, instructing, any day... yet I don't want that.

Why do I want Bomber Command?

Is it because I feel it my duty to go there? No, I don't think so.

Is it because I think I can do a better job there than anywhere else? Possibly that is something to do with it, though I have been assured many times that I should be far more usefully employed instructing. No, that is not the whole reason.

Is it because I feel that if I am killed I should not be missed? No, because I know that I should. True, I have no wife or children, but still, there are those who I know would miss me, and I am not hypocrite enough to think otherwise.

I think the real reason is that I feel so proud of Bomber Command, and all it stands for... that once more I want to associate myself with that name, and take part in its activities.

Winter came suddenly. Unlike in England, when the change is gradual and the seasons seem to overlap... when autumn can be like winter, and winter as mild as autumn, the Canadian Fall seemed to be very brief. It may have been that time was passing very rapidly, or the season may actually have been short... I don't know.

I do know this, though: I have never seen more brightly coloured leaves than I did on Prince Edward Island and in Ontario. They glowed with a brilliance I should not have thought possible, giving no indication of withering leaves, but rather of a fresh and flaming growth. Each wood and every tree was as bright and multi-coloured as any fire, with gold and scarlet, and all the myriad changes in between, showing their glory in a final orgy before they stood stark and frozen in the severe grip of snow and ice. Their flaming glory was a continual joy, and was in contrast to the fields of stubble and of brown earth all about.

The brilliance of colour did not last long. It was as though this daring splash was put on for a special occasion, and was too precious to be displayed for any length of time. The first cold winds shrivelled the leaves and tore them ruthlessly from the trees, leaving them dark and bare and dreary, rather like a house looks after the occupants have gone and it has been deprived of its furniture and treasures.

Prince Edward Island reminded me very much of England, with its small fields and hedges, and undulating country. It was a treat to see some green grass again, after the burnt, dried up, barren appearance of the prairies. Several fields, sheltered by trees along one side, might have been almost anywhere at home. Yet there was something lacking. There were no rabbits. If I could have seen some rabbits running up a bank, the illusion would have been complete.

The first snow started on November 16th, and I had the feeling that the natural ground was hidden for several months. I had seen the end of the snow when I arrived in Canada, and now I was witnessing the beginning.

I found it rather depressing, not at all like the first snow in England, which always somehow has a certain romantic and Christmassy feeling. It had that professional touch: it obviously knew its job, and intended to do it well!

The Australians and New Zealanders on the camp went crazy with excitement, rushing around collecting snowballs and hurling them at each other. It was the first time most of them had seen any snow. Those in the bedroom next to mine brought some into their room, forgetting it would melt!

I got some pleasure in the evening, with the light from uncurtained windows glancing on the sparkling whiteness. It was a sight I had not seen for some time, and was really beautiful.

I was wrong, however, about the snow coming to stay. We had a thaw, but it started to snow again in earnest on the last day of November, with a blizzard lasting about six hours. There was a foot of snow on the ground when it was over.

The walls of houses facing the wind resembled nothing more than a blank white surface, windows and doors being completely obscured. Cars left standing in the street were either buried in debris, or converted into huge snow mounds.

Nobody - at any rate the natives - seemed to take the slightest notice. Snow ploughs were on the roads almost as soon as the snow started, and the traffic seemed to be affected hardly at all.

I was waiting in a shelter with some friends, for a taxi, when one of the 'locals' asked me what I thought of it.

"I hate it," I said, and added: "I suppose this is about as bad as it can get?"

"My boy," he replied, "you haven't seen anything yet! Why, this is nothing. I recall, way back in 'twenty-four,' a guy came into the town with his horse and sledge, and the only place he could find to tether his horse was the top of the church steeple. Well, this guy, he went to the bootleggers, and was occupied for a couple of days. In his absence a thaw set in, and it seems he had forgotten all about his horse. When he came to collect it, he found it hanging from the top of the steeple!"

I was glad, in a way, to have experienced some real cold, when each breath you take hurts - it seems to fill your chest and throat with ice in a hard and painful grip; when the unwary can be frostbitten in a few minutes. I have seen a train travelling with the engine festooned with icicles, like a Christmas tree adorned with tinsel; I have stood under a shower and watched the steam freeze into a thick, opaque crust on the window pane; or seen water from a fire hose fall in lumps of ice before it reached the ground. That was real cold, and unpleasant cold.

When the wind was strong, at temperatures well below zero, every minute and every step outside was an ordeal. The snow blew from the ground like fine white sand: it blew up your trouser legs, and down your neck, and stung like red-hot needles.

It did not take long before a great deal of the wheeled traffic gave place to sledges. All horse-driven traffic was of this description, and it was a pleasant sight to see the silent horse-pulled sledge move slowly along the streets, with a bell jingling from the horse's neck. The driver sat swathed in layers of coats, and it only needed a red outer coat to make him look like Father Christmas. Nearly all prams discarded their wheels too, and put on runners instead.

Any form of walking on the roads or streets was hazardous, to say the least of it, and all school kids used to rush about on skates.

Everywhere we went we were pelted with snowballs, and I was thankful when the weather became sufficiently cold to make the snow too dry to gather into a ball. Not till then could we walk through the streets without expecting a snowball down the backs of our necks at any moment!

Before we left Canada, every family was collecting their Christmas tree. I believe there is hardly a household, no matter how small, or how old, who does not have a Christmas tree at Christmas.

Once again I found myself at , where I had started; only this time waiting to go home.

I went to the reception desk, and the Flight Sergeant in charge said: "Block Y... Room four... Bed three."

"How do you mean, *bed three*? How many beds are there?" I asked.

"We're a bit crowded, sir, but you'll find all the Flight Lieutenants will be together."

I certainly did! and the word *all* seemed to be right: we had those wretched double-decker beds that you find in Canadian camps. My neighbour was making his, and as he bumped his head on the top bunk for the fifth time, remarked:

"This is carrying democracy a little too far!"

I ran into a lot of my old friends, including Tony. He greeted me with: "What's cooking?"

His English was certainly improving!

Len was there, and as happy as a sandboy to be on his way home. It was good to see him again. He had completed his tour of instructing, and was all agog to get going on operations.

We were all thrilled at the prospect of going home, and impatient to get away. Every day irked. It seemed strange that after so many months - in some cases years - we should be kicking at a few extra days... but such is life. Home seemed very near, and it is not until you have been away for some time that you appreciate what a good place it really is.

Epilogue

And now once again I am at home, on leave again, and can look back on the past months as on something that is finished. By that I don't mean that my training is finished, but a phase, a fresh experience, is over. I ask myself, has it been worth while?... and I find the answer definitely yes. So far, I have got what I set out to get, and got what I wanted, which, to put it mildly, is pleasing.

The past months have been full months, and months well spent. Apart from the work point of view I have had a remarkably interesting, pleasant and enjoyable time. I have travelled, and seen parts of Canada I had not seen before, and made friends I should not otherwise have made... but, most important of all, I am eligible for the job I want more than any other.

People often say to me: *'Why do you want to go back on to operations? Surely you have done enough, and done your share!'* Has anyone done their share, and can anyone sit back contentedly until the job is finished? I know I can't. As for wanting to get back again, I know no one who has done one tour of operations who does not want to do another tour, and yet another. Call it the moth and the candle, if you like.

I know my friends and family feel that if I were to instruct I should be safe, yet one can't look on war in the light of lives. I suppose each one of us has got someone or other who thinks their loved one's life is the most important of all, yet there are only very few whose lives are so important that they cannot be sacrificed. You can't value a life, because it is the most valuable thing that exists. Yet lives have to be sacrificed by the million, in order that many million times more lives may be saved.

People sometimes criticize the pay of aircrews, how they don't get enough, and that their lives are worth more, yet can you value a life in terms of money? Of course you can't. A man may be getting fourteen, eighteen, twenty, thirty shillings or more a day, yet if he was getting thirty pounds a day, or three thousand pounds a day, would that be the value of his life? I know I should be offended if I thought my life was valued at a guinea a day! We are paid not for the value of our lives, but in terms of our skill and the extent of the training for our job.

It is a man's privilege to fight, and if necessary, die, for his country... and if he does die, he should not be mourned as lost, but rather should he be honoured as a saviour. His death should not bring sorrow; that would be a poor reward: it should bring gratitude and glory.

I always feel touched when my friends show solicitude for my future; touched, and rather pleased. I was talking to a country friend the other day, who said:

"Be you in the Air Force, then?"

I said I was.

"I hope you don't fly in they things?"

Postscript

Since this book has been finished and in the hands of the printers, there have been vast changes in my plans and hopes.

I am not in Bomber Command.

On my return home I found myself one of thousands - a pilot without a job: from the pilot's point of view galling, but from a broader aspect no doubt encouraging. There were thousands of us in the same boat, champing at the bit and itching to get cracking: yet there was no job for us. We were told we would eventually be posted to A.F.U.s and O.T.U.s and so on, but in the meantime we must be patient and await our turn.

I was one of the luckier ones, and given a job with the M.A.P., touring the country giving line shooting pep talks to factories - 'out of the blue to talk with you.' I was on this job for several months and it was fun - great fun, but not doing my flying much good!

Eventually I was given the option of transferring to the A.T.A.: the only other alternative being to stay where I was with no immediate prospect of a posting. I decided to take what was going and here I am ferrying in the A.T.A.; and the motto to this is, as the Queen in *Alice in Wonderland* would say, it's not much good counting your chickens before they are hatched!

Printed in the USA
CPSIA information can be obtained
at www.ICGtesting.com
LVHW051146120324
774239LV00004B/93